Globalization and International Political Economy

GLOBALIZATION

Series Editors
Manfred B. Steger
*Illinois State University, University of Hawai'i—Manoa,
and Royal Melbourne Institute of Technology*
and
Terrell Carver
University of Bristol

"Globalization" has become *the* buzzword of our time. But what does it mean? Rather than forcing a complicated social phenomenon into a single analytical framework, this series seeks to present globalization as a multidimensional process constituted by complex, often contradictory interactions of global, regional, and local aspects of social life. Since conventional disciplinary borders and lines of demarcation are losing their old rationales in a globalizing world, authors in this series apply an interdisciplinary framework to the study of globalization. In short, the main purpose and objective of this series is to support subject-specific inquiries into the dynamics and effects of contemporary globalization and its varying impacts across, between, and within societies.

Globalization and Culture
Jan Nederveen Pieterse
Rethinking Globalism
Edited by
Manfred B. Steger
Globalization and Terrorism
Jamal R. Nassar
Globalism, Second Edition
Manfred B. Steger
Globaloney
Michael Veseth
Globalization and Law
Adam Gearey
Globalization and War
Tarak Barkawi
Globalization and International Political Economy
Mark Rupert and M. Scott Solomon

Forthcoming in the Series
Globalization and American Popular Culture
Lane Crothers
Globalization and Militarization
Cynthia Enloe
Globalization and American Empire
Kiichi Fujiwara
Globalization and Feminist Activism
Mary Hawkesworth
Globalization and Labor
Dimitris Stevis and Terry Boswell

 **Supported by the Globalization Research Center at the University of Hawai'i, Manoa**

GLOBALIZATION AND INTERNATIONAL POLITICAL ECONOMY

The Politics of Alternative Futures

MARK RUPERT AND M. SCOTT SOLOMON

ROWMAN & LITTLEFIELD PUBLISHERS, INC.
Lanham • Boulder • New York • Toronto • Oxford

ROWMAN & LITTLEFIELD PUBLISHERS, INC.

Published in the United States of America
by Rowman & Littlefield Publishers, Inc.
A wholly owned subsidiary of The Rowman & Littlefield Publishing Group, Inc.
4501 Forbes Boulevard, Suite 200, Lanham, Maryland 20706
www.rowmanlittlefield.com

P.O. Box 317, Oxford OX2 9RU, UK

British Library Cataloguing in Publication Information Available

Library of Congress Cataloging-in-Publication Data

Rupert, Mark.
    Globalization and international political economy : the politics of
alternative futures / Mark Rupert and M. Scott Solomon.
        p.   cm. — (Globalization)
    Includes bibliographical references and index.
    ISBN 0-7425-2942-8 (cloth : alk. paper)—ISBN 0-7425-2943-6 (pbk. :
alk. paper)
        1. International economic relations.   2. Globalization—Economic
aspects.   3. Globalization—Social aspects.   4. Globalization—Political
aspects.   5. Capitalism.   6. Power (Social sciences)   I. Solomon, M.
Scott, 1968–   II. Title.   III. Series: Globalization (Lanham, Md.)
    HF1359.R87   2006
    337—dc22   2005009542

Printed in the United States of America

CONTENTS

ACKNOWLEDGMENTS

Given that this text is on globalization, it seems appropriate to acknowledge the contributions of various people and organizations around the world. Though this book has benefited from the advice, support, and criticism of a variety of scholars, activists, and policymakers, responsibility for any remaining faults rests with the authors.

In Hong Kong we'd like to thank Rex Verona and the staff of the Asian Migrant Centre, Bruce van Voorhis and Nick Cheesman of the Asian Human Rights Commission, Glenn Shive and the staff of the Hong Kong-America Center, and Professor Brian Bridges and the faculty and staff of the Department of Politics and Sociology at Lingnan University. In addition, Scott Solomon is grateful to the Lingnan Foundation for supporting his research in Hong Kong through the Lingnan Foundation Teaching Scholar program.

In Manila we'd like to thank Marla Asis and Fabio Baggio of the Scalabrini Migration Center, Liberty Casco and the staff of the Philippine Overseas Employment Association, Professor Stella Go of De La Salle University, Ildefenso Bagasao of the Economic Resource Center for Overseas Filipinos, and the staff of Unlad-Kabayan Migrant Services Foundation.

In the U.S. helpful comments and advice were provided by Abigail Augusta, Jonathan Bach, George DeMartino, David Gold, Phillip Kozel, Lily Ling, David Mitchell, and Richard Sherman. We would also like to acknowledge useful feedback provided by students and faculty at St. Olaf College, Bucknell University, and participants in the Leverhulme Foundation Conference on "Global Democracy, the Nation-State and Global Ethics," held at the University of Aberdeen, Scotland.

We have also benefited from the criticism and stimulation of graduate students of the Maxwell School at Syracuse University and the Graduate Program in International Affairs at New School University.

At Rowman & Littlefield, we have been the beneficiaries of the professional expertise and hard work of Jennifer Knerr and Renée Legatt. In addition to all of her other contributions to this project, Jennifer formulated a fitting and concise subtitle when we were unable to come up with one. Our series editors, Manfred Steger and Terrell Carver, have been patient, constructive, and helpful throughout this process.

Finally, we would like to acknowledge the unending support and understanding of our partners, Margot Clark and Bessie Skoures.

ABBREVIATIONS AND ACRONYMS

AMC	Asian Migrant Centre
ARAMCO	Arabian-American Oil Company
ATTAC	Association for the Taxation of Financial Transactions for the Aid of Citizens
BJP	Bharatiya Janata Party
COMELEC	Commission on Elections of the Philippines
DWU	Asian Domestic Workers' Union
EPZ	export processing zone
FMWU	Filipino Migrant Workers' Union
GATT	General Agreement of Tariffs and Trade
GDP	Gross Domestic Product
HM	historical materialism
ILO	International Labor Organization
IMF	International Monetary Fund
IMWU	Indonesian Migrant Workers' Union
IOM	International Organization for Migration
IPE	international political economy
IR	international relations
KRRS	Karnataka State Farmers' Movement
LDC	less developed country
MFMW	Mission for Filipino Migrant Workers
MNC	multinational corporation
MST	Movimento Sem Terra
NAFTA	North American Free Trade Agreement
NGO	nongovernmental organization
NIC	newly industrialized country

OFW	Overseas Filipino Worker
OPEC	Organization of Petroleum Exporting Countries
OWWA	Overseas Worker Welfare Administration
PAN	Partido Acción Nacional
PGA	People's Global Action
PNAC	Project for a New American Century
POEA	Philippine Overseas Employment Administration
PRD	Partido de la Revolución Democrática
PRI	Partido Revolucionario Institucional
TMC	techno-muscular capitalism
TNC	transnational corporation
TRIM	trade-related investment measure
TWA	Thai Women's Association
UNIFIL	United Filipinos
WEF	World Economic Forum
WSF	World Social Forum
WTO	World Trade Organization

INTRODUCTION

Our world is changing, and we are changing with it. The human beings who inhabit the various corners of the earth are becoming increasingly interconnected in all sorts of ways—economic, cultural, and political. Many people have come to use the term "globalization" as shorthand for all of this. Yet there is much controversy about what it all means. For many of its advocates, globalization represents progress on a world scale, the spread of free markets bringing with them economic rationality and efficiency, new opportunities, and the promise of materially richer and less arduous or insecure lives for increasing numbers of the world's people. In this view, those who resist globalization are an obstacle to progress and are harming all of us, but especially the people most in need of economic development.

Some critics of globalization see it as a threat to the sovereignty of their home country and to the special culture and way of life they associate with their national identity. For these nationalist critics, the appropriate response to globalization is to circle the wagons; keep alien peoples and their strange ways at bay; and reaffirm the bases of national economic, cultural, or racial identity. In the U.S. the political figure most strongly associated with this line of argument is Patrick Buchanan, but in numerous countries around the world political forces have emerged that oppose globalization because they fear that it will bring with it the erosion of their national identity.

Still others see in globalization a system for institutionalizing the power, privilege, and disproportionate wealth of the United States. Behind images of American-centered globalization, many see the heavy hand of U.S. global military power and wonder whether globalization is a new form of imperialism. In a related permutation, globalization appears as the im-

1

position of a Western, and especially American, cultural template upon the diverse communities and peoples of the world. Viewed from this perspective, globalization conjures images of a thoroughly commercialized and standardized mall-world, in which one finds the same set of Americanized chain stores, the same array of choices, wherever one goes, and traditional value systems and practices that cannot be mass-marketed on a global scale are discarded like yesterday's fashions.

To progressive critics and anticapitalists, globalization connotes not global progress so much as a heightening of the powers of corporate capitalists to pursue profit through the intensified exploitation of the earth's people and its natural environment. Sweatshops, domestic servitude, and toxic waste dumps for the many, juxtaposed with exclusive enclaves of fabulous luxury for the few, are the image of the future the current mode of globalization suggests for these critics. Some are then led to ask: How could we construct a different world, a different future, for ourselves and our children? Could more democratic and egalitarian forms of globalization be imagined? In the process of constructing a transnational culture of solidarity, mutual respect, and reciprocal responsibility, might we become new kinds of political actors, *citizens of the world* as much as of our home countries?

Far from being of purely academic interest, these different interpretations of globalization go to the heart of political struggles that will determine what kind of world we will live in, and what kinds of persons future generations may become. They are, in short, crucial to the politics of globalization.

Our argument in this book is that none of these views is entirely correct, but none is entirely mistaken. Globalization is a complex and contradictory phenomenon that encompasses progress and degradation, opportunity and compulsion, freedom and unfreedom. These various contradictions are points of political contestation, aspects of globalization around which various social groups may coalesce to struggle for realization of their vision of a future possible world. Which of these various tendencies will prevail, which potentialities will be realized and which will not, will be determined by the outcomes of these various struggles. While it is not possible to predict how these processes will play out, in this book we draw on the conceptual resources of historical materialism to sketch some of the more significant ways in which globalization is being contested and point toward some of the possible worlds that could emerge from the politics of globalization.

Introduction

Plan of the Book

In this book we argue that capitalist globalization—driven by boundless competitive accumulation and generating unprecedented time–space compression—is qualitatively distinct from other forms of extensive social interaction that may have preceded it. We highlight three distinctive features of globalizing capitalism. First, it has created the infrastructure of globalized production and finance, which together imply that the entire process of capital accumulation—from investment, to production, to sale of the product and reinvestment of surplus—is no longer anchored within the territorial bounds of particular nation-states. Second, we highlight the globalization of labor and new patterns of migration, which are directly linked to emerging transnational labor markets and the incipient deterritorialization of the state. Third, we emphasize the ways in which these processes of globalization have engendered new forms of political activity, the globalization of ideological struggle, as emergent transnational networks struggle over the meanings of globalization and the implications for future possible worlds. None of this should be construed as suggesting that nation-states no longer matter, for as we shall see, interstate politics remains an essential part of these global webs of economic, cultural, and political relations.

What kinds of social relations and entities are bound up with these processes of globalization, and where did they come from? What were the historical conditions of their emergence, and how have they developed and changed historically? What were the particular historical forms generated in the major eras of global capitalism, and what were the tensions and possibilities driving those forms toward change? In chapter 1 we highlight the ways in which theory matters for making sense of the politics of globalization. We lay the conceptual foundations for a critical analysis of contemporary capitalist globalization, arguing for the continuing relevance of historical materialism as a way to think about contested processes of social change. In chapter 2 we introduce the state and capitalism as historical social relations. We trace their interrelation through three major epochs of the world political economy: the nineteenth-century trading system, the Fordist hegemony of the mid-twentieth century, and the neoliberalism that emerged at century's end and has shaped the emergence of the twenty-first-century global economy.

In chapter 3 we begin to address some of the important ways in which globalization matters for our understandings of world politics. What new kinds of political processes, forms of organization, and actors are emerging in this new transnational context? What sorts of alternative possible worlds are projected by these new actors and their political imaginaries? How are their struggles and conflicts reshaping the politics of global governance? In this chapter we introduce the notions of transnational civil society and global governance structures and map their contestation and restructuring by such crucial new actors as the World Economic Forum, the rapidly growing sector of nongovernmental organizations (NGOs) and social movement groups, decentralized but coordinated networks of transnational resistance, and the alternative World Social Forum of Porto Alegre, Brazil.

How are such fundamental aspects of daily life as labor, home, and family changing under the pressures of globalization? In what sense are the politics of globalization "classed," "gendered," and "raced?" In chapter 4 we introduce notions of "intersectional politics" and use the case of Filipina domestic workers to illustrate the potentialities of transnational solidarity in a context of plural social identities. Transnational labor migration and the political organization of overseas domestic workers are transforming the nature of the nation-state in ways that deemphasize its territorial borders and hold the potential to create new forms of peripatetic "flexible citizenship."

Finally, in chapter 5 we directly address issues of neoimperial power lurking behind contemporary globalization. We ask how globalization and neoimperialism, militant Islamism, terror, and war on terror are bound up in contemporary global politics. We conclude with some reflections on the necessary open-endedness of the processes we have been reviewing, the political importance of alternative possible worlds, and the ideological visions that make them potentially accessible. Looking toward the future, we encourage hope while also underlining the importance of critical analysis and engagement. Throughout, our emphasis is on helping the reader develop a critical awareness of the politics of globalization and international political economy.

THE DIFFERENCE
GLOBALIZATION MAKES

What in the World Is Going On?

The evidence is everywhere, but what does it all mean? All around us we witness changes in global politics, in our work lives and consumption patterns, in the cultural products and ways of life we are exposed to. With dizzying speed new jobs and livelihoods are created in some places and destroyed elsewhere; buildings of superlative height spring up in cities around the world and the twin towers are suddenly brought low; new forms of political activism emerge that seem to transcend national boundaries, to empower and to terrorize people around the world. It is not always clear what these changes mean in terms of traditional political concepts. The politics of globalization are complex, are sometimes contradictory, and defy attempts to map political positions in terms of a simple left–right spectrum. So we have seemingly bizarre political spectacles in which "Teamsters & turtles" (i.e., labor unionists and environmental activists) can be seen with far-right reactionaries (nationalistic followers of Pat Buchanan, self-styled Christian patriots, even neo-Nazis) marching against neoliberal globalization in the streets of Seattle.[1] Movements resisting global neoliberalism have witnessed similar (uneasy) convergences be-tween the kinds of progressive, cosmopolitan forces traditionally associ-ated with the political Left, and conservative nationalists traditionally associated with the Right, in Australia, Austria, Britain, France, Germany, Sweden, Venezuela, and elsewhere.[2]

We observe something almost invariably called an "antiglobalization" movement, which at its core comprises many who call not for autarky (i.e., self-sufficiency and minimal trade) but for "fair trade" entailing greater eq-uity and sustainability, unions who call for transnational solidarity instead of a "race to the bottom" in competition with "foreign" workers, and the absence of anything like the traditional centralized political leadership to clarify all of this by defining a party line. In short, the "antiglobalization" movement is largely called into being by one form of globalization but calls for another.

Still another symptom of the confusion reigning in these debates is the notion that one must determine whether, on balance, globalization is good or bad, progressive or exploitative, and the concomitant casting of asper-sions on those who think differently about these issues. Among the advo-cates of *neoliberal globalization* (that is, globalization understood primarily in terms of the economic logic of liberalized trade and financial flows) it is common to dismiss those unappreciative of the logic of free trade theory as "flat-earthers" or worse.[3] For their part, many critics of the predominant form of globalization do not hesitate to paint it as unambiguously evil, hyperexploitation of people and the environment driven by nothing more complex than greed. Vast numbers of people around the world equate globalization with Americanization and resent the arrogance, power, and privilege this represents. So, what in the world is going on?

Part of the explanation stems from the use of different categories people use when analyzing globalization. Obviously, the state is a central part of the story of globalization but is not the only object of inquiry available. Indeed, the possibility of moving capital (whether in the form of finance or factories) across state boundaries with little friction can potentially un-dermine the sovereign powers of states and hence has been a central part of the globalization debate. This same movement of capital has led some to question whether it is possible to identify a national economy at all and to the more general question "Who is *us*?" when we speak about national policies designed to benefit a national economy.[4] Globalization requires an analysis that looks both within and across states in determining how the various processes identified with it create winners and losers and new forms of both economic and political power.

Another part of the explanation for the confusion surrounding attempts to describe globalization in Manichean terms rests with the difficulties various intellectual traditions have had in theorizing capitalism as a form of social organization. Our reading of historical materialism suggests that capitalism is simultaneously exploitative and progressive, creates both wealth and poverty, and brings into being forms of freedom and unfreedom, power and powerlessness. In a word, our understanding of capitalism is *dialectical*,[5] and our understanding of globalization is as the continuation and intensification of a long-standing process, the internationalization of commodity production and capital accumulation. Therefore, we approach globalization as a dialectical process that provides plenty of evidence for its indictment as well as its praise. Our task is an explication of how we got to this particular kind of world and how we might envision other possibilities.

At the most abstract level, globalization can be understood in terms of "time–space compression"; the eminent geographer David Harvey defined time–space compression as entailing drastic changes in material life and ways of thinking, "processes that so revolutionize the objective qualities of space and time that we are forced to alter, sometimes in quite radical ways, how we represent the world to ourselves."[6] Manifestations of such changes are the dramatically reduced transportation times for goods and people moving around the world, the impact of telecommunications and the Internet, and even the rapidity with which cultural artifacts become globally accessible commodities. An American consumer in Iowa can purchase a product made in China by a German company whose toll-free number connects the buyer to a customer service agent in India. An investor can trade securities or speculate in foreign exchange markets twenty-four hours a day by sitting at her computer and successively accessing markets in New York, London, and Tokyo. The same twenty-four-hour cycle can enable computer code to be continuously written as globally distributed work groups hand off the project at the end of one team's day and the beginning of another's. Bootleg DVDs and knockoff T-shirts featuring the latest animated Disney characters appear in Asian markets almost as soon as the actual film hits American theater screens. Anti-American protest posters in Pakistan feature images, downloaded from the Internet, of Osama bin Laden with a satirized Sesame Street Muppet ("evil Bert") scowling over his shoulder. Anecdotal evidence of these sorts is often cited to demonstrate that globalization represents an epochal shift from what preceded it.

While it is undeniable that significant changes have occurred in the global political economy, we should be careful about drawing overly dramatic conclusions from seemingly unprecedented time–space compression. Nearly one hundred years ago the English economist John Maynard Keynes made these observations about the form of time–space compression evident in the early twentieth century:

> The inhabitant of London could order by telephone, sipping his morning tea in bed, the various products of the whole earth, in such quantity as he might see fit, and reasonably expect their early delivery upon his doorstep; he could at the same moment and by the same means adventure his wealth in the natural resources and new enterprises of any quarter of the world, and share, without exertion or even trouble, in their prospective fruits and advantages; or he could decide to couple the security of his fortunes with the good faith of the townspeople of any substantial municipality in any continent that fancy or information might recommend. He could secure forthwith, if he wished it, cheap and comfortable means of transit to any country or climate without passport or other formality, could despatch his servant to the neighboring office of a bank for such supply of the precious metals as might seem convenient, and could then proceed abroad to foreign quarters, without knowledge of their religion, language, or customs, bearing coined wealth upon his person, and would consider himself greatly aggrieved and much surprised at the least interference.[7]

Clearly, the time–space compression evoked by Keynes's passage was remarkable for his era. But can we date such time–space compression to the globalization of the late British Empire and/or technological innovations of the turn of the nineteenth century? Some seventy years before Keynes wrote the above, other observers noted the forces driving time–space compression characteristic of their own era:

> The bourgeoisie, by the rapid improvement of all instruments of production, by the immensely facilitated means of communication, draws all, even the most barbarian, nations into civilization. The cheap prices of commodities are the heavy artillery with which it batters down all Chinese walls, with which it forces the barbarians' intensely obstinate hatred of foreigners to capitulate. It compels all nations, on pain of extinction, to adopt the bourgeois mode of production; it compels them to introduce what it calls civilization into their midst, i.e., to become bourgeois themselves. In one word, it creates a world after its own image. . . . The bourgeoisie, during its rule of scarce one hundred years, has created more massive and more colossal productive forces than have all preceding generations together. Subjection of nature's forces to man, machinery, application of chemistry to industry and agriculture, steam navigation, railways, electric telegraphs, clearing of whole continents for cultivation, canalization of rivers, whole populations conjured out of the ground—what earlier century had even a presentiment that such productive forces slumbered in the lap of social labor?[8]

So, which era of time–space compression is definitive? How can we identify the moment when time–space compression produces the revolutionary change that Harvey suggests? An important clue is the difficulty of finding similar observations that predate the eighteenth or nineteenth century. To be sure, we could find historically important events influenced by people far away (e.g., the advancement and spread of philosophy, science, and mathematics through the Islamic communities, which ranged from Iberia to the Indonesian archipelago, and which helped to jump-start the European Renaissance). We would not, however, find examples of globally significant time–space compression as profound, rapid, and dramatic as that reflected in the passages quoted above. The reason is that all other forms of social organization and production pale in comparison to the dynamism and productivity of capitalism. No other form of social organization in history has been capable of such dramatic change because no other form was based on private production in competition with other producers, the surplus from which was plowed back into ever-more-competitive production. Previous forms of social organization and production of human needs were based on some form of hierarchically defined systematic end or goal, some social standard of "enough." Capitalism is unique in that for the first time in human history we live within a system of social organization that has no goal, no end, other than limitless accumulation for its own sake. We discuss this characteristic of capitalism further below.

If the birth of capitalism—beginning in Northwest Europe in the eighteenth century and eventually spreading globally—serves as a historical marker that sharply divides social epochs, and we believe it does, then what does that mean for the understanding of globalization? How do we make sense of the undeniably dramatic changes that have occurred in the last several centuries? If we attempt to answer such questions by relying on empirical measures of globalization (e.g., ratios of exports + imports/ GDP, volume of foreign exchange trading, and the like) we will be compelled to make choices about what these measures mean. We argue that a systematic approach is required to make sense of the bewildering amount of empirical evidence available to scholars of globalization. In short, *theory* is necessary to guide us in making these choices. In fact, theory is not only necessary but unavoidable. Deciding which variables matter, which measures to take, which are significant and which are trivial, and even deciding that measurement is important, are all decisions that flow from a theoretical perspective, however conscious we are of the precise elements that perspective contains. There is no neutral position from which to weigh evidence on these matters, because the selection of evidence itself requires a theoretically derived position from which to do so, a position that provides us with a set of criteria and a frame of reference in terms of which we can select and make sense of evidence. We argue for the enduring relevance of the tradition of historical materialism (HM) as providing a compelling—if not necessarily final or complete—understanding of the process of globalization.

Globalization: Theory Matters

Within the academy the concept of "globalization" is often viewed as problematic, frequently pilloried as a "buzzword" devoid of meaning, or concomitantly, attributed with so much meaning there seems little in the world that is not represented, affected, or determined by globalization. Interestingly, what makes something a "buzzword" is frequent invocation in popular discourse. Even if globalization has been grossly exaggerated, defined poorly, and/or invoked carelessly, it is clear that *something* is going on that causes academics, policy makers, the press, and the public as a whole to continually resort to using the term. What in the world is going on? Before we can attempt to answer this question, we must address another: How can we think and speak about what in the world is going on? What conceptual vocabulary—what *theory*—can help us make sense of the changes occurring in our world?

We attempt to make sense of globalization by recourse to the intellectual resources of international political economy (IPE) and the (too often overlooked or misrepresented) critical tradition of HM. International political economy is a diverse field of study that resists simple summary. In the scholarly mainstream, a common definition of IPE is the study of how states and markets interact and how these interactions involve both conflict and cooperation. Mainstream scholars of IPE have generally conceived of these interactions as embodying a conflict of two opposing logics.

The first logic is that of interstate politics. Mainstream IPE scholars point to an anarchic system of multiple sovereign states, each of which claims to be the supreme political authority within its own territory and among which, as a consequence, there can be no higher authority—that is, no global government that can authoritatively resolve disputes among sovereign states. It is in this sense that the interstate system is "anarchic." This "sovereignty-anarchy" vision of the world is analogous to the lawless "state of nature" conceived by early-modern English philosopher Thomas Hobbes as an unregulated war of each person against all others. In terms of this analogy, the insecurity endemic to the interstate system gives rise to a brute Hobbesian logic that compels states to maximize their wealth and power relative to other states to minimize their vulnerability to coercion or conquest. In terms of this "zero-sum" logic, one can attain safety and security only to the extent that one's wealth and power exceed that of potential rivals: Any relative gain for a competitor or rival is perceived as a diminution of one's own security.

On the other hand, mainstream IPE scholarship understands the market as the virtual antithesis of such nasty and brutish interstate politics. Rather than seeing the world in terms of zero-sum competition in which nice guys finish last (or don't finish at all), the world economy is understood in terms of a Smithian logic of market-based cooperation. Following Adam Smith—the Scottish liberal philosopher and founder of modern economics—this logic suggests that there is much to be gained from a social division of labor in which producers specialize in whatever activity they do best and, to satisfy all their other needs, exchange with other specialized producers through the mediation of the market. Due primarily to efficiency gains made possible by specialization and driven by market competition, the total output of society will be much greater in a market-based social division of labor than if each participant attempted to be entirely self-sufficient by producing everything for himself or herself. According to this classical liberal logic, it is this inducement of an improved real standard of living that leads rational, self-interested individuals into market-based relations that are voluntary, cooperative, and mutually beneficial. The same basic logic is applied to trading relations among states. In contrast to the zero-sum Hobbesian logic, in which one state's relative gain is a menace to others, Smith posits a world in which market-mediated cooperation holds out the possibility of making trading partners better off *together*. Although modified and updated in various ways, this insight continues to constitute the core of international economic theory.[9]

To its credit, IPE as a scholarly tradition resists the impulse to characterize the modern world as straightforwardly representative of one simple logic and focuses its attention on the very tensions that define modernity—the putative separation of social life into politics and economics, public and private, state and society. However, despite our admiration for the ways in which IPE begins to raise questions about the interrelation of politics and economics in the modern world, we find that mainstream IPE has a monumental blind spot that prevents it from fully realizing the potential implications of this questioning. Mainstream IPE tends not to see the ways in which the world of states and the world of markets actively produce one another and constitute a single, if contradictory, whole. So, to take one glaring example, it is common for IPE scholars to identify politics with power struggles among states—struggles that may be affected by the ways in which wealth is distributed in the economy—but rare for them to ask in what ways the economy is *itself political*, constructed on the basis of power relations intrinsic to the economy—and how these economic power relations in turn affect not just interstate politics but the very nature of states themselves. This blind spot is important because it (mis)leads us into thinking of the world of states and the world of markets as two given entities that may affect each other marginally but whose existence in their current form—characterized by either purely political or purely economic logic—is taken for granted. This assumption in turn makes it difficult if not impossible to pose questions about fundamental changes in these sets of social relations and ways in which the future of social life might be fundamentally different from the past. To remedy this essentially static vision, we draw on historical materialism—the scholarly tradition inaugurated by Karl Marx and extended in a variety of directions by subsequent scholars and political activists.

Historical materialism has generally been neglected as a source of critical theoretical leverage in the IPE literature. On the one hand this may seem surprising, given that the very questions that often vex IPE are also at the center of HM, albeit with radically different assumptions about the historical contingency of states and markets as well as the role scholars should play in these debates. On the other hand, it is not surprising that a tradition such as HM, with a quite conscious commitment to a politics of human emancipation and a critical posture toward the status quo, should be viewed by mainstream political science as insufficiently "objective" and therefore "unscientific." In response to such challenges it seems only fair to ask: How "objective" is mainstream IPE research? Specific research questions in IPE, as a subfield of political science dominated by American political scientists, have generally mirrored the concerns confronting U.S. policy makers. For example, on the heels of the U.S. defeat in the Vietnam conflict and amid questions of the declining relative power of the U.S., IPE was preoccupied by the theory of hegemonic stability, which generally argued that a stable global economic and political order among capitalist states was best served by the leadership of one overwhelmingly preponderant state, which would shoulder most of the burdens involved in constructing and sustaining an open, liberal world order. To say the least, this was a convenient scientific finding in a political context in which the U.S. was struggling to maintain its post–World War II position of international leadership and privilege. And likewise now that the Cold War has ended and the U.S. is the sole remaining superpower, mainstream American political science is infatuated with the so-called Democratic peace thesis, arguing that "democratic" states—which happily seem to resemble the U.S. in all relevant regards—rarely if ever make war upon one another, so that a world of democratic states (equivalent perhaps to a collection of Uncle Sam clones) would be the most peaceful and prosperous possible world. Again, an argument politically useful to the world's preeminent power emerges from a tradition of scholarship that insists on its own scientific objectivity. And, as Ido Oren has thoroughly documented, such cases are hardly exceptional but are rather instances of an historical pattern in the evolution of mainstream American political science.[10] In contrast to self-serving doctrines of scientific objectivity that exempt mainstream political science from critical political examination, we suggest that the theoretical traditions of these scholars of international relations (IR) and IPE have *some* relationship to the political, economic, and cultural milieu in which they are produced.[11] Given the Panglossian flavor of these self-consciously scientific arguments, it is surely not surprising that critical scholarly traditions, like HM, confront these dominant scholarly traditions with the response that this is *not* the best of all possible worlds; that this world is in the process of changing in potentially fundamental ways; and that predominant ways of thinking about world politics, international economics, and IPE may not help us understand and shape these processes.

Historical Materialism and a Critique of Globalizing Capitalism

Deeply enmeshed in intellectual and political projects spanning well over a century and much of the world, historical materialism—the tradition of "practical-critical activity" founded by Karl Marx, often used interchangeably with "Marxism"—defies reduction to any simple doctrine or single political position. Nevertheless, it is possible to understand this constellation of intellectual and political positions as constituting variants of HM insofar as they are animated by a critique of capitalism, understood as a particular historical form of organization of human social life, rather than as a natural or necessary expression of some innate and invariant human nature. Without pretending to speak for the whole of Marxism, we present here a particular synthetic interpretation of historical materialism and its relevance for global politics.

Contrary to the simple-minded caricatures that retain in some quarters a measure of academic currency—for example the claim that in Marxism economics determines politics, or that it speaks only to domestic social relations and has little to say about world politics—HM has focused its attention on capitalism as a material way of life, an ensemble of social relations that has never been coterminous with "the economy" as we know it in the modern world, nor with the so-called domestic sphere putatively

13

contained within the boundaries of the sovereign state. Marxism has much to say about historically evolving structures and practices that have crossed national boundaries and linked the domestic and the international, the economic and the political—much to say, in short, about the social production of global politics. Historical materialism suggests that states and systems of interstate and transnational power relations are embedded in and (to a significant degree) produced through systems of relations that encompass (among other things) the social organization of production. This latter is itself structured according to relations of class (and, many contemporary Marxists acknowledge, by race and gender as well as other relations of domination) and is an object of contestation among social classes, state managers, and other historically situated political agents. Thus politics is not confined to the formally public sphere of the modern state but permeates the economic sphere as well; just as the state and interstate politics can profoundly shape economic and social life, so the politics of the economy can have enormous implications—not generally recognized within the terms of mainstream worldviews—for the historical form taken by particular states and world orders constructed among states. The point here, it must be emphasized, is not to reconstruct global politics on the basis of an economistic reductionism in which a foundational economic sphere is understood as the fundamental cause of human social phenomena, a sort of universal independent variable, but rather to argue something very nearly the opposite—that politics and political struggle are essential aspects of the processes by which all social relations and structures are (re)produced, and hence that the analytical separation of political from economic life—as well as domestic and international aspects of these—represents a false dichotomy that obscures much of potential political importance.

Historical materialism begins from the premise that humans become what they are in large part because of the social forms through which they organize their material reproduction, a process which is at once both natural and social. Human social beings continually (re)produce the conditions of their existence through socially organized productive activity, which, because we are human and not animals, necessarily involves thinking, speaking, planning, and organizing together. Through this process, the material world, social relations and ideas, and human beings themselves are continuously reproduced or transformed. Thus, to paraphrase Marx, people make their own history and in the process determine what it means to be human in a particular sociohistorical context, but they cannot just make themselves anew, de novo, in any way they please. Rather, historically situated social agents—whose actions are enabled and constrained by the social relations and self-understandings that constitute their identities—inherit particular social forms from preceding generations and proceed to (re)produce, alter, or transform the social world in which they find themselves situated. In *The German Ideology*, Marx distinguishes the process-oriented view characteristic of historical materialism from other ways of understanding social life: "As soon as this active life-process is described, history ceases to be a collection of dead facts as it is with the empiricists . . . or an imagined activity of imagined subjects, as with the idealists."[12] No longer need we understand the world as a collection of apparently objective facts mutely confronting and constraining us, nor is the only alternative to imagine our world and ourselves as the creation of some mystical superhuman subject; rather the material-social world as it exists for us may be understood as a human social product, and since we are ourselves integral to that world, we are—potentially—capable of social self-determination in and through our socially organized productive activity. Under historical circumstances of capitalism, our inability collectively to determine the social organization of our productive activity, the kind of society we will live in, and the kinds of people we will become, is for Marx an index of our unfreedom. In the guise of capitalist private property, Marx wrote, "Man's own deed becomes an alien power opposed to him, which enslaves him instead of being controlled by him."[13]

Capitalism as Marx represents it is not a seamless web of oppression or an inescapable black hole of political despair, but rather a contradictory life of "dual freedom." In such a dialectical Marxian view, capitalism entails liberation from the relations of direct politico-economic dependence (such as the simultaneously political and economic subordination of the serf to the feudal lord) characteristic of precapitalist forms of social life. Instead of being born into—and destined to live our entire lives within—precapitalist politico-economic hierarchies, the emergence of capitalism undermines these hierarchies and presents possibilities for social individuation (the sense that one is one's own master and can succeed or fail based on one's own merit and effort) and "political emancipation" within republican forms of state (securing individual rights and liberties for citizens). But capitalism simultaneously limits the historically real emancipatory possibilities it brings into being by (re)subjecting individuals to social domination through the compulsions of market dependence: Everyone must somehow acquire the money necessary to purchase the necessities of life, and for the vast majority who are not already wealthy this translates into a compulsion to sell their labor-power to a capitalist employer to "make a living." Further, to the extent that capitalist market relations appear to us as beyond our control, simply the way things are and must be, we surrender our collective social authorship of society and instead treat it as if it were an objective fact to which we must adapt ourselves. Evoking comparison with religious cults who manufacture objects of worship (fetishes) and then bow down before them as if they were gods, Marx referred to capitalism's reification of social power relations—that is, the social division of labor congealed into the apparently objective form of commodities—as "fetishism."[14]

These dialectics of freedom and unfreedom, the powers they generate and resistances they engender, have produced families of capitalist historical structures fraught with tension and possibilities for change. Whether any such possibilities are realized, and in what particular ways, depends on open-ended political struggles in which the power relations of capitalism will necessarily be implicated. One of the enduring insights of Marxian theory is that the seemingly apolitical economic spaces generated by capitalism—within and across juridical states—are permeated by structured relations of social power deeply consequential for political life and, indeed, for the (re)production of social life as a whole. These powers may be ideologically depoliticized—and thus rendered democratically unaccountable—in liberal representations separating a naturalized and privatized economy from the formally political sphere of the state (recall here Adam Smith's vision of the market economy as voluntary, cooperative, and mutually beneficial). The operation of this economy (and the implicit social powers residing within it) may then be represented as something approaching a universal social good, the engine of economic growth, and a generalized prosperity. However, another of these enduring Marxian insights is that social power relations are also *processes*—dynamic, contradictory, and contestable.

The critical leverage of a Marxian critique of capitalism is generated by its explicit focus on the social power relations that inhere in, and yet are obscured by, the structures and practices of capitalist production and exchange. Under historical conditions of capitalism, social relations are mediated by things—commodities. Although the social division of labor under capitalism has brought together and collectively empowered human producers as never before, capitalism simultaneously divides and disables them by representing their social relations as naturalized relations of exchange between commodities (again we encounter Marx's famous concept of the "fetishism of commodities"). To the extent that social relations are subsumed into a world of putatively independent objects—"things"—communities of human producers are correspondingly disempowered. This involves both our material social lives and the ways in which we understand ourselves and the social world: "The social world of capitalism

16

appears as something we inhabit . . . rather than some of the ways we are, and it is this estrangement of the real content of social life that grounds the abstractions which come to stand in for it: modernity's representations . . . of both society and self."[15] Inhabitants of the capitalist market, the subjects of capitalist modernity, are represented to themselves as abstract (i.e., atomistic, asocial) individuals who, as such, are largely unable to discern— much less communally to govern—the social division of labor in which they are embedded. The social division of labor takes on the appearance of objectivity, an uncontrollable force of nature, the mystical market whose price signals and compulsions individuals neglect at our peril. Concomitantly, capitalism's fetishism and reification serve to mystify social power relations by making power appear as a property of *things* that may be possessed (or not) by abstract individuals. As Marx put it:

> That which exists for me through the medium of *money*, that which I can pay for, i.e., which money can buy, that *am I*, the possessor of money. The stronger the power of my money, the stronger am I. The properties of money are my, the possessor's, properties and essential powers. . . . Through money I can have anything the human heart desires. Do I not therefore possess all human abilities? Does not money therefore transform all my incapacities into their opposite? . . . What I as a man cannot do, i.e., what all my individual powers cannot do, I can do with the help of *money*.[16]

The implications for democracy are deeply ironic. For even as capitalism realizes "political emancipation" through the development of the liberal republic in which citizens are formally equal under the law, it effectively reifies, privatizes, and depoliticizes class-based social powers (by associating them with ownership of capitalist "private property") and thereby evacuates from the purview of political democracy much of the substance of social life, hollowing out democracy's promise of social self-determination.

Behind these mystifications, capitalist social relations generate the possibility of asymmetrical social powers distributed according to class. Socially necessary means of production are constituted as private property, exclusively owned by one class of people. The other class, whose exclusion from ownership of social means of production is integral to the latter's constitution as private property, are then compelled to sell that which they do own—labor-power, their capacity for productive activity—to gain access to social means of production and hence—through the wage—their own means of survival. As consumer of labor-power, the capitalist may control the actual activity of labor—the labor process—and appropriate its product, which is then subsumed into capital itself as part of the process of accumulation. As a consequence of their position within the social organization of production, then, capitalists may exercise two kinds of social power.

As *employers*, capitalists and their managerial agents attempt to assert control over the transformation of labor-power—the abstract, commodified capacity for labor—into actual labor. Driven by the imperatives of competitive accumulation, they seek to maximize the output of workers in relation to wages paid for labor-power and may lengthen the work day or transform the labor process itself (intensifying labor and increasing its productivity) to do so. This latter tendency was manifested in struggles surrounding Fordist workplace regimes (as we shall see in chapter 2).

The second social identity through which capitalists are socially empowered is as *investors*. Deciding when, where, and how to invest is a prerogative attendant on ownership of private property in the means of production. As owner-investors, capitalists routinely make decisions that directly determine the social allocation of labor and resources—the pace of aggregate economic activity and the shape of the social division of labor—and indirectly limit the scope of public policy through the constraint of "business confidence" and the implicit threat of "capital strike" or transnational capital flight. If a state fails to maintain conditions supportive of "business confidence," or if it enacts policies that appear threatening to the interests of the owning class, investors responsible only to their own pocketbooks may decline to invest there. In effect, they may subject the state to a "capital strike": driving up interest rates, depressing levels of economic activity, throwing people out of work, exacerbating the fiscal problems of the state, and endangering the popular legitimacy of the incumbent government. Every politician from whatever party understands that economically distressed voters are unhappy voters, and that the politician's ability to hold office therefore depends on avoiding the loss of business confidence. This disciplinary power has the effect of prioritizing the interests of investors, who are as a class effectively able to hold entire states/societies hostage without having to conspire or threaten.[17] Their collective power is built into the system. Thus are market values enforced upon governments that claim to be responsive to popular democratic pressures. In the concise summary of critical political economists Sam Bowles and Herb Gintis, "The presumed sovereignty of the democratic citizenry fails in the presence of the capital strike."[18]

Insofar as the social powers of capital are effectively privatized— associated with private ownership and exchange of property among legally equal individuals in an apparently depoliticized economic sphere—they are ideologically mystified and democratically unaccountable. Antidemocratic and disabling as they might be, however, these class-based powers are neither uncontestable in principle nor uncontested in fact. Like all relations of social power, capitalist power relations are reciprocal, constituting a "dialectic of power" subject to ongoing contestation, renegotiation, and restructuring. The reproduction of these powers is always problematic and must be politically secured on an ongoing basis in particular contexts. Successful reproduction of class power is hardly assured.

However, the process of challenging these powers may be significantly more complex than more fundamentalist versions of Marxism have been prepared to contemplate. For class powers must be actualized in various concrete sites of social production where class is combined with other socially meaningful identities operating in those historical circumstances. Capitalist power over wage labor has been historically articulated with *gendered* and *raced* forms of power: separation of workplace from residence and the construction of ideologies of feminized domesticity rationalizing unpaid and underpaid female labor, ideologies of white supremacy rationalizing racial segregation and white privilege, gendered and raced divisions of labor, and so forth. Indeed, these relations of race and gender have had important effects on class formation, with dominant classes repeatedly using race and gender to fragment the working class and prevent the emergence of a unified class-based political movement. This implies that in concrete contexts class cannot be effectively determining without itself being determined. However, this is not to say, in some pluralist sense, that class is only one of a number of possible social identities, all of which are equally contingent. Insofar as productive interaction with the natural world remains a necessary condition of all human social life (as Marx maintained), we suggest that understandings of social power relations that abstract from the social organization of production must be radically incomplete. To the extent that capitalism and its putatively private relations of power organize crucial parts of social life on a transnational scale, the struggles surrounding these relations and their various articulations in sites around the world merit serious study as part of the question of global power and resistance.

If Marx left us with incisive theorizations of capitalism, its core structures and contradictions of freedom/unfreedom, it was the Italian political theorist and communist leader Antonio Gramsci who contributed to the historical materialist tradition a conceptual vocabulary with which to understand and enable ideological struggles and processes of transformative politics. Marx suggested that socialist transformation might emerge out of the confluence of capitalism's endemic crisis tendencies, the polarization of its class structure and the intensified exploitation of the proletariat, and, most important, the emergence of the latter as a collective agent through the realization of its socially productive power, heretofore developed in distorted and self-limiting form under the conditions of concentrated capitalist production. Gramsci accepted in broad outline Marx's analysis of the structure and dynamics of capitalism but was unwilling to embrace the more mechanical and economistic interpretations of Marx circulating in the international socialist movement. Contrary to the dogma of vulgar Marxism, Gramsci believed progressive social change would not automatically follow in train behind economic developments but must instead be produced by historically situated social agents whose actions are enabled and constrained by their social self-understandings, that is, by ideology. Thus, for Gramsci, political power is more than just the force that emerges (as Mao once said) out of the barrel of a gun; rather, power entails a continuously shifting balance of coercion and popular consent. To the extent that consensual forms of power—organized through ideologies effectively anchored in "popular common sense"—predominate over coercion in a given historical situation, Gramsci spoke of hegemonic power, or hegemony. In such a Gramscian view, then, popular common sense becomes a critical terrain of political struggle. His theorization of a social politics of ideological struggle—which he called "war of position" to distinguish it from a Bolshevik strategy of frontal assault on the state—contributed to the historical materialist project of dereifying capitalist social relations (including narrowly state-based conceptions of politics) and constructing an alternative—more enabling, participatory, intrinsically democratic—social order out of the historical conditions of capitalism.

For Gramsci, popular common sense could become a ground of struggle because he saw it as an amalgam of historically effective ideologies, scientific doctrines, and social mythologies. He understood popular common sense not as monolithic or univocal, nor was hegemony an overwhelmingly dominant ideology that simply shut out all alternative visions or political projects. Rather, common sense was understood to be a syncretic historical residue (he used the geological metaphor of successive layers of sedimentation to convey this), fragmentary and contradictory, open to multiple interpretations, and potentially supportive of very different kinds of social visions and political projects. And hegemony he understood as the unstable product of a continuous process of ideological struggle, "war of position," "reciprocal siege." Gramsci's political project thus entailed addressing the popular common sense operative in particular times and places, making explicit the tensions and contradictions within it as well as the sociopolitical implications of these, to enable critical social analysis and transformative political practice.[19]

Beginning with the seminal work of Robert Cox, Gramscian concepts

20

have been deployed by scholars of world politics (not all of whom would be at home with the label "Marxist") seeking to counter the predominant intellectual climate of state-centric atomism and its deeply conservative implications. Drawing on the relational and process-oriented conceptual underpinnings of HM, Cox stressed the historical construction of various forms of state in the nexus between social forces (classes, social movements, and other collective social agents) on the one hand, and world orders on the other. He stressed that this relational nexus necessarily involves economic, political, and cultural aspects, all of which are bound up with systems of power that are not coterminous with sovereign states. And drawing on Gramsci's conceptualization of hegemony, Cox suggested that these systems of power could be meaningfully distinguished depending upon the relative balance of coercive and consensual forms of power.[20] The rethinking of world politics produced by Cox and other neo-Gramscian scholars has provided a critical alternative to conventional understandings that take sovereign states—understood as territorially based wielders of coercive power—to be an unproblematic given, the essential reality, at the heart of world politics. From our perspective, then, the concepts developed by Marx, Gramsci, and Cox are crucial to a critical rethinking of international political economy and the politics of globalization.

We have seen that globalization is not an entirely new phenomenon since transnational time–space compression is as old as capitalism and is defining of modernity. However, long before capitalism emerged there were imperial forms of political systems that could be thought of as early forms of globalization. The Greek, Roman, Byzantine, Muslim, and Ottoman empires certainly exhibited a reach that at times affected much of the "known" world. The Aztec, Incan, and Mayan empires in what we now call Latin America, as well as those in what we now call China and the Indian subcontinent, demonstrate that territorially extensive empires with effective communications, trade, and cultural diffusion are not uncommon in human history. In fact, it would be difficult to identify any point in human history at which isolated, self-contained communities existed with negligible interaction. Long-distance travel and trade, accompanied by cultural and technological exchange, are not exceptional in recorded history. From this fact it may be tempting to conclude that what we now call globalization is just more of the same—perhaps even evidence of some innate characteristic of human beings such as the "propensity to truck, barter, and exchange" suggested by Adam Smith.[21] However, such a conclusion would be a mistake, and to see why we need to pay special attention to the motivation for past forms of globalization/imperialism.

Before the onset of capitalism and its distinctive social relations, empires were based on territorial acquisition by military force. While this generalization arguably oversimplifies previous forms of empire and may mask significant distinctions among them, it is certainly the case that, whatever distinguished empires from one another, their enforcement was based on a logic of military superiority and territorial expansion. Though the movement of goods and the payment of tribute were common to many early forms of empire, they were not primarily based on a capitalist logic in which competitive accumulation compels the continual transformation of production processes.[22] Contemporary globalization is distinctive because it is indeed based on such a capitalist logic and is, as a consequence, transforming the social organization of production—along with finance, migration patterns, and much else besides—on a transnational basis. Despite these novel features, contemporary globalization is not innocent of military expansion or a politics of coercion. We discuss at length the "neoimperial" aspects of contemporary globalization in chapter 5; for now, suffice it to say that globalization is fraught with relations of social power, some of which can be directly connected to a project of U.S. global supremacy. The politics of globalization entail new social power relations of transnational scope, powers that exhibit economic, political, and cultural dimensions, and our project in this book is to interpret the political contests surrounding these new global powers in terms of a Marxian-Gramscian politics of coercion and consent.

Although not without its tensions and limitations, Marxian theory provides critical leverage for understanding the structures and dynamics of capitalism, its integral if complex relationship to the modern form of state, the class-based powers it enables, and the resistances these entail; Gramsci's rich legacy suggests a conceptual vocabulary for a transformative politics in which a variety of anticapitalist movements might coalesce to produce any number of future possible worlds whose very possibility is occluded by capitalism. In the present context of globalizing capitalism and neoimperialism, such resistance has taken the form of a transnational confluence of movements for global justice and peace. It contains elements that are explicitly class-identified but also encompasses a rich variety of social forces opposed to the depredations of globalizing neoliberal capitalism and the arrogant U.S. power that enforces it. Insofar as the multifarious movements for global justice and peace inhabit common ground, it is a world where massively unequal wealth and divergent life chances are underpinned by historical concentrations of both economic and military power, an implicitly undemocratic world that, while historically real, is neither natural nor necessary. In their diverse but convergent challenges to this concentrated power, these movements embody a rejection of capitalism's essentially self-interested individuals in favor of more relational and process-oriented visions of social reality, an affirmation that social life can and does change in important ways and that human beings are capable of living together in a rich variety of ways. To the extent that they are forging a transnational culture of solidarity across meaningful social differences and together effect resistance to the power relations that variously and commonly oppress them, they may represent the germ of a transformative political process that need not be contained by capitalism's reified separations of economics/politics, state/society, domestic/international.

But such progressive forces are not alone in contesting neoliberal globalization. Reactionary nationalist forces have arisen worldwide to reassert particular cultural, ethnic, or racial identities in the face of global change and to attempt to anchor these identities firmly in the popular common sense of their target populations: from American "patriot" militias to British skinheads, followers of Jean-Marie Le Pen in France, Jörg Haider in Austria, Pauline Hanson's One Nation movement in Australia, and the Hindu nationalist Bharatiya Janata Party (BJP) in India. Further, and even more ominously, we may be witnessing the emergence of bloody new forms of transnational conflict in which resistance to the disproportionate U.S. power and privilege embodied within globalization generates repeated episodes of terror and counterterror, a nascent Islamist insurgency waged by the most radical members of the international Muslim community and its worldwide diaspora corresponding with neoimperial deployments of American military might. The politics of globalization are indeed complex and contradictory, offering new possibilities both exciting and dreadful.

A BRIEF HISTORY OF GLOBALIZATION

In some senses globalization may be an extremely old phenomenon, and other writers—depending on the theories in terms of which they understand the world—may suggest continuities between contemporary globalization and historically expansionist episodes, among which they might include the empires of the Greeks, Romans, Persians, and Islamic Arabs, the transoceanic explorations of the imperial Chinese navy, the Spanish Conquistadors, or still others. However, as we explained in the previous chapter, we follow the tradition of historical materialism to identify those aspects of modern capitalist globalization that are qualitatively distinct, historically unprecedented, and world-transforming. Insofar as its central dynamic is the competitive drive for boundless accumulation, capitalism compels market-dependent capitalists to continually seek out new profit opportunities on an ever-broader scale and with ever-increasing intensity. If a particular capitalist fails to do so, or simply doesn't do so quickly enough, he or she will be vulnerable to competition from other capitalists and may well be driven out of business. It is through generalized market dependence, the relentless competitive pressures it generates, and the continual reconstruction of social relations it enables, that modern capitalism

25

has produced the dramatic time–space compression that we recognize as characteristic of contemporary globalization. Viewed from this perspective, then, the history of contemporary globalization is bound up with—if not entirely reducible to—the history of capitalism.

Contrary to Adam Smith, who saw the roots of capitalism in what he supposed was an innate human characteristic, the "propensity to truck, barter, and exchange one thing for another," we are persuaded by scholars who locate the roots of capitalism in an historical social transformation that started by changing relations of agricultural production in one small corner of the world and ended up generating industrial revolutions, dizzying technological change, globalizing production and finance, emerging transnational labor markets, and, not incidentally, relations of power and domination that now encompass most of the world.[1] Although our brief overview cannot do justice to the historical and political complexities, we must stress that none of this was predestined; it did not occur automatically, as a result of mechanisms internal to capitalism which, once set in motion, ground out their inexorable result. Rather, this history is the story of myriad ongoing social struggles required to (re)subject persons and their social lives to the disciplines of capital and the social powers imputed to private property. The apparent triumph of globalizing capitalism is, at its core, a political story, and one that is far from finished. One of the central messages of this book is the essential open-endedness of human social life and the importance of critical theory in helping us to recognize possibilities for remaking our world. But before we can come to grips with the politics linking the present with the future (which we do in subsequent chapters), we need to sketch out the historical path that brought us to where we are.

Capitalism, Modernity, and Globalization

Much conventional wisdom identifies capitalism with trade, then traces the latter from the great trading cities of the early modern era deep into the mists of human prehistory. But this has the disabling effect of making capitalism appear as natural, inevitable, and analogous perhaps to processes of natural selection and biological evolution (indeed this very analogy animated Social Darwinist thinking). We can no more change capitalism, this line of reasoning suggests, than we can alter the fact that we walk on two legs or draw oxygen without the aid of gills. To the extent that we persuade ourselves of this, the political future of capitalism is bright indeed, and its exploitation and unfreedom will go unchallenged. Capitalist hegemony will have been secured.

If there are political grounds for resisting the ideological equation of capitalism with trade in general, so too are there historical reasons. For the trade that existed prior to the emergence of capitalism was generally trade in luxury goods—reflecting the merchants' logic of buying low and selling high—rather than the generalized market dependence characteristic of a thoroughly commodified society. The latter entails relentless competitive pressure to improve labor productivity and therefore to continually transform the social organization of production—a hallmark of capitalism and a key feature distinguishing it from other ways of organizing society, and that predisposes it toward globalization. To the extent that we identify capitalism with any kind of trade whatever, we lose sight of this important distinction.

On political and historical grounds such as these, the eminent Marxist theorist Ellen Wood argues against identifying capitalism with trade and suggests instead that it involved a fundamental and far-reaching social transformation:

> Perhaps the most salutary corrective to these assumptions and their ideological implications is the recognition that capitalism, with all its very specific drives of accumulation and profit maximization, was born not in [urban trading centers] but in the countryside, in a very specific place, and very late in human history. It required not a simple extension or expansion of barter and exchange but a complete transformation in the most basic human relations and practices, a rupture in age-old patterns of human interaction with nature.[2]

The age-old patterns to which Wood refers are various forms of peasant-based agriculture in which producers (the peasants) had direct access to the land and implements necessary to grow crops. Dominant classes, who lived off the surplus labor of the peasants (i.e., additional productive work beyond that required for the material sustenance of the peasant families themselves), could extract this surplus only by "extra-economic means—that is, by means of direct coercion, exercised by landlords or states employing their superior force, their privileged access to military, judicial, and political power."[3] In other words, where producers had direct access to the necessary means of production, dominant classes had to resort to political-military means to impose taxes or rents and thereby extract surplus labor and reproduce their social position of domination. As a consequence, under these circumstances the relationship of political-economic domination that obtained between classes was there for all to see, a direct and daily presence in social life. Insofar as economic exploitation was inseparable from political-military domination, there was no socially meaningful distinction to be made between what the modern world refers to as the political and economic aspects of life. The rupture that changed this relation of production and surplus appropriation effectively gave birth to capitalism and, through it, to the forms of social life we associate with modernity and globalization.

The crucial rupture first occurred in the English countryside, where from the late seventeenth to early eighteenth centuries a unique constellation of factors—including the emergence of an effective central state and highly concentrated landholding by the post-feudal nobility—combined to create the germ of a new social world. As the English state consolidated and subsumed the political-military powers formerly wielded by landed nobility under more feudal arrangements, "the relatively weak extra-economic powers of landlords meant that they depended less on their ability to squeeze more rents out of their tenants by direct, coercive means than on their tenants' productivity."[4] As both landlords and tenants became increasingly market-dependent, landlords could demand and receive increasing monetary rents from agricultural producers who would not otherwise be able to gain access to land. This in turn meant that only those tenants who "improved" the land to increase productivity could maintain their land tenancy from year to year. "In this competitive environment, productive farmers prospered and their holdings were likely to grow, while less competitive producers went to the wall and joined the propertyless classes."[5] While acknowledging the role of legally enforced enclosures (transforming into exclusive private property what had been common lands to which peasant producers had customary rights of access), Wood argues that

> market imperatives certainly accelerated the polarization of English rural society into larger landowners and a growing propertyless multitude. The famous triad of landlord, capitalist tenant, and wage-laborer was the result, and with the growth of wage labor the pressures to improve labor productivity also increased. The same process created a highly productive agriculture capable of sustaining a large population not engaged in agricultural production, but also an increasing propertyless mass which would constitute both a large wage-labor force and a domestic market for cheap consumer goods—a type of market without historical precedent. This is the background to the formation of English industrial capitalism. The effect of market imperatives was to intensify exploitation in order to increase productivity.[6]

With the transformation of precapitalist political-economic exploitation into the market-based and seemingly apolitical compulsions of capitalism, the explicitly political, coercive powers underlying the social organization of production faded into the background, no longer a direct and daily presence in economic life, displaced by the impersonal forces of market competition. Once this separation went into effect, regular and obvious exercises of direct coercive force were no longer necessary for dominant classes to extract surplus labor from producers. Rather than the sharp point of a sword, capitalism routinely relies upon what Marx famously called "the dull compulsion of economic relations," the relentless pressure in a commodified society to earn enough to secure the material necessities of life:

> The organization of the capitalist process of production, once fully developed, breaks down all resistance. The constant generation of a relative surplus-population keeps the law of supply and demand of labor, and therefore keeps wages, in a rut that corresponds with the wants of capital. The dull compulsion of economic relations completes the subjection of the laborer to the capitalist. Direct force, outside economic conditions, is of course still used, but only exceptionally. In the ordinary run of things, the laborer can be left to the "natural laws of production," i.e., to his dependence on capital, a dependence springing from, and guaranteed in perpetuity by, the conditions of production themselves.[7]

The emergence of capitalist wage relations involved changes in gender relations as well. Michelle Barrett pointed toward the ways in which the emergence of capitalism altered the gender relations of the "family-household system" by separating the place of residence and consumption (that is, the home) from the site of work (now defined predominantly as waged labor, sold to an employer outside the home). Concomitant with this separation came the ideological construction of women as domestics and caregivers, situated, for the most part, within the home and therefore largely dependent upon male wage earners. The culturally established expectation that women will be supported by fathers or husbands has served to rationalize substandard pay for those women who do seek employment outside the home. "The family-household system has resulted in the 'double shift' of wage labor and domestic labor for many working class women, and the assumption of their household dependence has left many 'unsupported' women in a very vulnerable position."[8] This division of the labor force by gender has been politically consequential not just for the disempowerment of women, but also for the working class as a whole. Gendering the division of labor in these ways has meant the relative privileging of male workers and the concomitant assignment of women disproportionately to the ranks of the poorly paid and the insecure. This gendered division, which produces predominantly female "cheap labor" and intensifies competitive pressures among working people, makes it more difficult to realize possibilities for a politics of solidarity that might escape the "dull compulsion" of economic life under capitalism.

Concomitant with the rise of market dependence and the separation of direct coercive force from economic life that this entailed was the development of a new form of political authority that could appear to be separate from economic life—the root of modern, republican forms of government claiming to be representative of citizens in general rather than a direct extension of the power of the dominant class. "In England, there was a clearer separation between the political, coercive powers of the state and the exploitative powers of the propertied classes which derived their wealth from purely 'economic' forms of exploitation. So the private economic powers of the ruling class did not detract from the political unity of the state, and there was both a centralized state and an integrated national economy."[9] This proved to be an earthshakingly potent combination, and as capitalism and the modern political state developed together in England, enormous competitive pressures were brought to bear upon the rulers of other states, who found themselves disadvantaged in rivalry with England. "States still acting on pre-capitalist principles of trade, or geo-political and military rivalry hardly different in principle from older, feudal conflicts over territory and plunder, would be driven by England's new competitive advantages to promote their own economic development in similar ways."[10] In other words, capitalism and the social forms of modernity that came into being along with it—the modern political state and market-dependent economic life centering around the exploitation of waged labor—very soon created pressures for the transformation of social relations (both economic and political) on a geographically expanding scale. In sum, capitalism, modernity, and globalization have been historically bound up together.

Capitalism and Imperialism

The possibility of imperialism is built into the historical social relations that constitute the core of capitalism. Recall from our previous discussions that capitalism entails a structural separation between the economic and political aspects of social life—that is, the depoliticization and privatization of the economy, which makes possible capitalist private property and compels those who are not members of the owning class to sell their labor-power to survive. This structural separation implies that the state in a capitalist context is generally dependent upon the economic activities of capitalists—private investors and employers—to generate enough economic growth and employment within its territory to legitimate the government and the social order as a whole and to produce resources the state can tax so as to fund its operations. The state has, therefore, a compelling interest in the overall success of accumulation—that is, private profit reinvested in the growth of capitalist enterprise—by capitalists whose operations are based within its territory. But since capitalist economic activity routinely overflows the juridical boundaries of particular nation-states, the imperatives of capitalist market competition and geopolitical competition among states may converge to generate imperialism—the deployment of military power in the service of capital accumulation.

Capitalist imperialism—as distinct from precapitalist tribute-extracting or commerce-controlling empires—has involved the use of coercive power to create and maintain conditions necessary for capitalist production, exchange, and investment (together constituting the process of capital accumulation) to occur on a transnational scale.[11] This has entailed forcibly integrating new areas into the world market, destroying noncapitalist ways of life and commodifying social relations (i.e., creating widespread market dependence), generating an exploitable "proletarianized" labor force (a class of people who do not own any "means of production" and therefore must sell their labor-power), and enforcing the dominance of private property and capitalist access to important resources. This is not to say that all modern instances of imperialism have had a purely capitalist character—as a consequence of the globally uneven development of capitalist social relations we may identify historically hybrid instances such as King Leopold's Belgian Congo around the turn of the nineteenth century, where partial commodification was attended by outright extortion and the massive and ruthless exercise of coercive force to compel hyperexploited labor at the cost of (literally) millions of lives.[12] Perhaps the most (in)famous instance of imperialism, the British Raj in India, also evolved along hybrid lines, initially representing little more than a massive trading monopoly and evolving into a militarily enforced imperial state, strangling the Indian textile industry to make way for industrially produced English textiles and forcibly extracting taxes from the rural peasantry.

However, viewed from a world-historical perspective, Wood argues, the global expansion of capitalist social relations over the last two centuries has prepared the way for the recession of explicitly political coercive force into the background of global capitalism, never entirely absent but not as a rule directly present or visible in economic relations. Global capitalism then relies less on naked imperial power and more on the authority of local political states legally to secure private property and enable accumulation to proceed through apparently apolitical market mechanisms. When conditions of transnational accumulation have been more or less secured, capitalism can function without ongoing recourse to directly coercive exploitation; rather, it relies primarily upon "the dull compulsion of economic relations." In this view, the contemporary capitalist world represents a "mode of economic domination managed by a system of multiple states," for "neither the imposition of economic imperatives nor the everyday social order demanded by capital accumulation and the operations of the market can be achieved without the help of administrative and coercive powers much more local and territorially limited than the economic reach of capital."[13] When local states and ruling classes are unable or unwilling to maintain the political conditions of transnational accumulation, imperial coercive force may be brought out of the closet to reimpose those conditions.

British Capitalism and the Nineteenth-Century World Order

Like Portugal, Spain, and Holland before it, England had been an old-fashioned, precapitalist imperial power throughout much of the early modern period, using military force to control resources and dominate trade overseas, enrich the kingdom and its merchants, and finance still greater military power. This was consistent with "mercantilism"—the doctrine of using state power to promote national commercial advantage, increase the country's balance of payments surplus (the excess of income from exports sold abroad over expenditure on imports), and thus enhance its relative wealth and power in competition with rival states. However, by the nineteenth century, capitalism was firmly established in Britain, the world's first industrial revolution was well underway, and the mercantilist political economy based on protecting domestic industries and sending militarized monopoly companies to colonize overseas territories was about to be challenged in the first attempt to construct a liberal international economic order. This was an important precursor to the twentieth-century liberal order, which fostered the emergence of contemporary capitalist globalization.

Early in the development of capitalism, the pioneering liberal economist Adam Smith undercut the intellectual rationale of mercantilism when he published his masterpiece, *An Inquiry into the Nature and Causes of the Wealth of Nations* (1776). Smith argued that in its preoccupation with money, mercantilism had misunderstood the very nature of wealth and was, therefore, quite literally counterproductive. Instead of obsessing over trade balances and accumulation of treasure as the mercantilists had, Smith argued that real wealth had more to do with a nation's ability to produce goods and services and thereby support a higher material standard of living. This, in turn, was directly related to the extent to which division of labor had been enacted in that society:

> It is the great multiplication of the productions of all the different arts, in consequence of the division of labor, which occasions, in a well-governed society, that universal opulence which extends itself to the lowest ranks of the people. Every workman has a great quantity of his own work to dispose of beyond what he himself has occasion for; and every other workman being exactly in the same situation, he is enabled to exchange a great quantity of his own goods for a great quantity . . . of theirs.[14]

The solution to Smith's puzzle of why some nations are wealthy and others poor he found in division of labor, for it is that which enables producers to specialize in a particular branch of activity and to develop more fully the particular abilities associated with that specialization. An economy of multiple specialized producers is vastly more productive than if each person attempted to be entirely self-sufficient (producing all necessary goods for himself or herself). With division of labor, each specialized producer is able to trade his or her surplus production for that of others, so that he or she benefits from the special abilities of *all* producers cooperating together in the market-mediated economy. The greater the extent of division of labor, the greater the total output of goods and services—the stuff of real wealth—available to society. And since specialized producers must exchange their surplus output for that of others to satisfy all their various material needs, division of labor and market exchange go together in this Smithian world. Accordingly, Smith argued that free markets and trade were crucial parts of the puzzle of social wealth. This conclusion was no less valid for international economics. He therefore condemned mercantilism—which had supported protection of a nation's domestic industry and attempts to secure international trading monopolies, and thereby interfered with free trade, specialization, and increasingly extensive division of labor—as intrinsically inefficient and unable to generate real social wealth. In light of its subsequent influence on the development of the capitalist world economy, Smith's argument against mercantilist policies of protectionism is worth quoting at length:

> To give the monopoly of the home market to the produce of domestic industry, in any particular art or manufacture, is in some measure to direct private people in what manner they ought to employ their capitals, and must, in almost all cases, be either a useless or a hurtful regulation. If the produce of domestic can be brought there as cheap as that of foreign industry, the regulation is evidently useless. If it cannot, it must generally be

hurtful. It is the maxim of every prudent master of a family never to attempt to make at home what it will cost him more to make than to buy. The tailor does not attempt to make his own shoes, but buys them of the shoemaker. The shoemaker does not attempt to make his own clothes, but employs a tailor. The farmer attempts to make neither the one nor the other, but employs those different artificers. All of them find it for their interest to employ their whole industry in a way in which they have some advantage over their neighbors, and to purchase with a part of its produce, or what is the same thing, with the price of a part of it, whatever else they have occasion for.

What is prudence in the conduct of every private family can scarce be folly in that of a great kingdom. If a foreign country can supply us with a commodity cheaper than we ourselves can make it, better buy it of them with some part of the produce of our own industry employed in a way in which we have some advantage. The general industry of the country, being always in proportion to the capital which employs it, will not thereby be diminished, no more than that of the above-mentioned artificers; but only left to find out the way in which it can be employed with the greatest advantage. It is certainly not employed to the greatest advantage when it is thus directed towards an object which it can buy cheaper than it can make. The value of its annual produce is certainly more or less diminished when it is thus turned away from producing commodities evidently of more value than the commodity which it is directed to produce. According to the supposition, that commodity could be purchased from foreign countries cheaper than it can be made at home. It could, therefore, have been purchased with a part only of the commodities, or, what is the same thing, with a part only of the price of the commodities, which the industry employed by an equal capital would have produced at home, had it been left to follow its natural course. The industry of the country, therefore, is thus turned away from a more to a less advantageous employment, and the exchangeable value of its annual produce, instead of being increased, according to the intention of the lawgiver, must necessarily be diminished by every such regulation.[15]

In short, when a nation adopts policies of protectionism it harms itself in two related ways. First, protectionism prevents it from benefiting from the special abilities of other producers who can produce many of the goods it needs more efficiently and cheaply than it can itself. Second, protectionism forces it to reallocate its own labors away from that which it does best and toward things it does less efficiently, needlessly expending its scarce resources. In both ways, the nation's real material standard of living is lower under protectionism than it would be under an open system of specialization and trade. Smith's was the first sophisticated theorization of a liberal economic order, based on specialized production and free market exchange.

Intellectual arguments cannot become socially dominant, however, without favorable material conditions and political agents to enact them. As capitalism began to develop in Britain and generated the world's first industrial revolution, a new class of wealthy manufacturers emerged to challenge the political power of the landowning nobility. These manufacturers and their political allies embraced liberalism and its doctrine of free markets in order to overcome the agricultural protectionism that benefited British agrarian elites but resulted in higher food prices, and hence higher labor costs for employers in manufacturing, than might otherwise obtain. In 1846, these liberalizing capitalists scored a historic political victory with the repeal of the "Corn Laws," as Britain's agricultural tariffs were known. Subsequently, British manufacturers sought to gain access to the markets of other countries, where the superior productivity resulting from Britain's industrial revolution would enable them to compete effectively. Beginning in 1860, the British negotiated a series of bilateral trade treaties lowering tariff barriers with major trading partners. International monetary stability—necessary for traders to be confident of their ability to bring home the profits from international transactions—was provided by the adoption of a gold standard: Britain and several of its major trading partners agreed to link their currency values to gold and to allow inflows and outflows of gold in response to trade imbalances (i.e., if one country bought more from the rest of the world than it sold to them, it would pay the balance in gold). And British investors sent their capital throughout the world, famously contributing to the construction of railroads such as those that soon spanned North America. With provisions for freer trade and monetary stability and the growth of international investment, the first liberal international economic order came briefly into being. It is important to note that this early liberal system was in many ways imperfect and uneven, neither comprehensive nor global in its scope—for example, Britain maintained its empire and certainly did not practice free trade in important colonial possessions such as India, and the United States declined to liberalize trade and continued to protect its growing industries throughout the nineteenth century. Nonetheless, the British-centered liberal economic order is a significant precursor of the twentieth-century capitalist world order that has generated contemporary globalization.[16]

The nineteenth-century liberal order lasted relatively briefly. British industrial supremacy was increasingly challenged, and international competition intensified, as Germany and especially the U.S. were undergoing their own economic transformations, developing new kinds of industrial systems. The U.S. overtook Great Britain—the home of the first industrial revolution—to assume the mantle of the world's most productive economy sometime during the 1890s, and further widened its advantage in overall productivity through subsequent decades as it began to develop Fordist forms of industrial production.[17] The depressions that struck the international economy in the late nineteenth century triggered a turn back toward nationalism, protectionism, and imperialism among Britain's European trading partners, while the British themselves began to reemphasize their imperial trading relationships.[18] By the end of World War I, which left Britain economically exhausted and indebted, the U.S. was clearly the world's most dynamic capitalist economy.

Fordist Capitalism and the Twentieth-Century World Economy

Capitalism underwent major institutional transformations during the twentieth century, and the story of capitalist globalization, we believe, cannot be adequately told without taking account of these changes and their implications. At the core of these institutional changes was the emergence of Fordism—understood here as a social system of mass production and consumption entailing political and cultural, as well as economic, relations. As you might guess, the system was named after the famous inventor and industrial entrepreneur Henry Ford. That much of the story is fairly well known, but there is much about Fordism that is less well known—the conflictual conditions of its emergence, its wider social and political significance, and the ways in which its evolution has been bound up with globalization. Here we summarize our interpretation of that complex and important story.

In Highland Park, Michigan, during the winter of 1913–1914, Henry Ford and his staff of industrial engineers began to combine some new and some established production technologies into an integrated system centering on mechanized, moving assembly lines. Taken as a whole, Ford's system of production had the effect of intensifying the industrial power and discipline exercised by management over workers that had been envisioned by the "scientific management" movement. Also known as Taylorism, this earlier series of attempts to restructure industrial production had its roots in the highly publicized work of industrial engineer Frederick W. Taylor and his disciples, who between 1890 and 1915 developed and preached the doctrines of scientific management to maximize the productivity of labor. Taylor and his disciples divided the production process into a series of distinct tasks, each of which might be performed by a particular worker. Each worker's job was further subdivided into a series of specific micro-tasks, then "scientifically" reordered so as to minimize time and motion required to complete each job. The worker was then instructed how and when to move each part of his body in the execution of management-specified work routines. Taylor famously likened these scientifically managed workers to "trained gorillas" who could be made as productive as possible through the organization and discipline offered by his system. In effect, Taylorism promised industrial capitalists that they could displace self-directing, skilled laborers from production via the division of the production process into a series of micro-tasks, strictly scripted and timed by management and executable by less-skilled, less-expensive, more readily interchangeable and controlled industrial workers. Taylorism, then, represents a landmark in the long capitalist process of "deskilling" labor, transferring power over the actual conduct of work from workers to management to obtain the maximum possible output per hour of waged labor.

Fordism represented another crucial landmark in this process. To achieve, on a massive scale, something like Taylor's vision of managerial power and control, Fordism incorporated specialized machinery, producing precisely standardized, reliably interchangeable parts that could be easily assembled by relatively unskilled workers. Further, Ford's industrial engineers pioneered the functionally sequential arrangement of machines and operations within the factory so that the production process could become a smooth one-way flow in which the product moved progressively closer to completion as it moved from one workstation to another along the production line. Finally, Ford integrated production flows of various subcomponents into converging, mechanized assembly lines, the speed of which could be controlled by management.

Fordism had the effect of dramatically enhancing the power of employers over the production process, enabling management to control flow of production and the pace and intensity of work. In the mid-1920s, one production worker described the relentless and strenuous effort that his job required, and the consequences of failing to meet that standard on a daily basis, as follows: "You've got to work like hell in Ford's. From the time you become a number in the morning until the bell rings for quitting time you have to keep at it. You can't let up. You've got to get out the production . . . and if you can't get it out, you get out."[19]

Whereas Smithian-inspired liberalism sees the economy as a sphere of apolitical, voluntary, and mutually beneficial cooperation, HM enables us to see relations of power operative within the capitalist economy. At the core of the Fordist reorganization of production was the construction of new relations of power in the workplace; to the extent that these relations of power could become established parameters of the work process, capital would reap the gains of manifold increases in output per hour of waged labor. The promise of massive increases in productivity led to the widespread imitation and adaptation of Ford's basic model of production through the industrial core of the U.S. economy, and in other industrial capitalist countries, where Fordism was imitated under the competitive pressures of increasingly internationally active U.S. firms.

Despite its tantalizing appeal to industrial capitalists, however, Fordism was plagued by serious problems, which can be understood only through analysis of the politics of production. Fordist industrial organization promised enormous productivity gains *if* workers could be induced to consent to, and cooperate with, the new organization of production. Securing the ongoing consent of workers was critical, since the vast, interdependent systems of production Fordism required could be disrupted if workers at any single point failed to perform assigned tasks in the prescribed ways at the expected times. This was hardly guaranteed, and in fact worker consent was deeply problematic due to the repetitive, exhausting, dull, and degrading nature of work under the authoritarian Fordist production system. In this context, workers were unmotivated at best and often resistant to management power and the dehumanizing system of production it sought to impose. This political problem intrinsic to Fordist production was not easily resolved, and over a period of decades industrial capitalists resorted to a variety of strategies to secure their control over the industrial workplace. This dialectic of workplace power and resistance produced recurrent episodes of intense and sometimes violent class-based struggle through the first half of the twentieth century.[20]

Difficult as it was, Fordism's political problem of consent was not altogether intractable and by mid-century had been ameliorated (if not resolved) through the rise of industrial unions and their recognition as legitimate bargaining agents by both the U.S. state and industrial capitalists. The unions' demonstrated ability to wield the strike weapon—that is, collectively to withhold labor—compelled government and employers to accept collective bargaining as the price of industrial peace and continued production. Following decades of struggle, this mutual accommodation was effectively ratified with the landmark 1950 contract between General Motors Corporation and the United Auto Workers—the famous "Treaty of Detroit." Among its provisions, the union recognized and pledged to respect management's authority to organize production and make investment decisions. In return, management agreed that real wages (that is, wages in relation to prevailing price levels, hence reflecting workers' actual material standard of living) would be directly linked to productivity growth so that workers could enjoy a share of the fruits of their (increasingly productive) labor. This contract set the pattern for major collective bargaining agreements across the industrial core of the U.S. economy.

Overall, industrial peace was secured, the productivity gains promised by Fordism were increasingly realized, and productivity and real wages grew more or less in tandem from the 1950s into the 1970s. In the decades after World War II, large numbers of blue-collar industrial workers could afford to join the growing middle class of American "consumers." Combined with the emergence of mass advertising, which encouraged consumers to fill their homes with the latest "new and improved" products, and consumer credit, which enabled middle-class households with a reliable income stream (i.e., a steady job) to purchase homes, automobiles, furniture, and appliances, a mass production–mass consumption economy was emerging. As U.S.-based, Fordist-organized firms exported and invested overseas, they set new competitive standards of productivity in the world economy. Fordist modes of organization were adopted, adapted to local conditions, and spread throughout the industrial core of the global economy.[21]

During the postwar decades, government policy sought to maintain the macroeconomic balance between mass production and consumption. Following the doctrines of British economist John Maynard Keynes, fiscal policies (levels of taxation and government spending) and monetary policies (governing money supply and interest rates) were used to promote generally higher levels of economic growth, employment, and income. Such Keynesian-inspired, growth-oriented policies were common across the industrial capitalist countries during these decades. This common, progrowth orientation was facilitated by the international economic institutions constructed under the political leadership of the U.S. in the wake of World War II. Serving the interests of the U.S. government and American industrial capitalists by creating a postwar world friendly to American-style Fordist capitalism, correspondingly less receptive to the potentially subversive influence of Soviet-style communism, and open to U.S. goods and investment, these institutions sought to foster international economic growth through a stable international monetary system and open trade.

Even before the war had ended, official representatives of forty-four nations under the leadership of the U.S. and Britain were convened at Bretton Woods, New Hampshire, to begin designing the postwar world economy. The Bretton Woods agreements (1944) established the U.S. dollar as "key currency" for the postwar world economy, effectively guaranteeing its value by backing it with gold at a fixed price ($35 per ounce of gold). Since U.S. dollars were as good as gold, traders located in countries around the world could confidently accept dollars in payment for goods and services sent across international borders, and this confidence was crucial to the postwar expansion of international trade. Also at Bretton Woods, the International Monetary Fund (IMF) was created to provide credit to those countries whose balance of trade and investment income with the rest of the world were in deficit. For countries in such a deficit situation, the pre-Keynesian orthodoxy of the nineteenth century had prescribed bitter medicine: an economy-wide lowering of consumption and real standards of living, thereby decreasing imports (since people could no longer afford as many imported goods) and cheapening exports (since labor and other costs would be lower in a recessionary economy), and sacrificing economic growth to rebalance international income and payments. However, according to the new Keynesian-inspired thinking, IMF credit would enable countries in such a situation to sustain economic growth and minimize recessionary belt-tightening by borrowing the international funds required to finance their deficit. The increasingly international mass production–mass consumption economy would not then be endangered by regular bouts of recession as countries sought to rebalance their international accounts. Finally, the World Bank was also created at Bretton Woods, originally intended to finance the reconstruction of the world economy out of the rubble left after World War II had ended. Together, the U.S. dollar as key currency, the IMF, and the World Bank formed the three pillars of the international monetary system for the postwar world, collectively referred to as the Bretton Woods system.

After the Bretton Woods agreements had constructed the basis of a stable world monetary system, the infrastructure of a liberalized trading system was created. The first task on the trade agenda was the reduction of tariffs. A tariff is a tax imposed upon imported goods as they cross the border, making imports more expensive in relation to domestically produced goods. This has the effect of protecting domestic producers of particular goods from foreign competition but makes those goods (and others as well) significantly more expensive for consumers and (according to Smithian-inspired liberal views) reduces the overall level of productivity and growth in the world economy. The General Agreement of Tariffs and Trade (GATT) provided a framework for a series of rounds of multilateral tariff reduction that encouraged the rapid growth of international trade. The initial round of tariff reductions in 1947–1948 involved twenty-three countries, but by the 1994 Uruguay Round of GATT, 123 participants agreed to collectively reduce barriers to international trade. As a consequence of successive GATT-sponsored rounds of multilateral trade liberalization, the average tariff level in the world economy fell from nearly 40 percent in 1947 to under 5 percent in 1994. Correspondingly, over the second half of the twentieth century the volume of world merchandise trade expanded dramatically, with trade outpacing the growth of global economic output—implying that increasing proportions of world economic activity involve trade.[22]

The project of liberalizing world trade has expanded well beyond the multilateral negotiation of tariff reductions. In 1995, as a result of the Uruguay Round agreement, the GATT was succeeded by the World Trade Organization (WTO), a permanent organization with unprecedented powers of surveillance and enforcement over a range of trade-related policies enacted by member states. This reflects a broadening of the agenda of liberalization beyond tariff reduction to encompass "harmonization" of (formerly "domestic") rules and regulations governing business insofar as these appear, from the liberal perspective, as potential nontariff barriers to trade.[23] Encouraging rapid growth in international trade and investment and intensifying the competitive dynamics that generate time–space compression, this internationalization of a Fordist-Keynesian, growth-oriented capitalism contributed mightily to what we would now recognize as the early stages of globalization. However, postwar Fordism was plagued by difficulties, which by the late twentieth century led to its supercession by a form of capitalism we call global neoliberalism.

From Fordism to Global Neoliberalism

The first major factor contributing to the strains on the Fordist world economy was an increase in the intensity of competition in world markets for manufactured goods.[24] As the economies of Europe and Japan recovered from the devastation of World War II and adapted Fordist production to their own local conditions, their manufactured exports became increasingly competitive in world markets. Further, the traditional colonial division of labor—in which dominant countries produced manufactures and their current or former colonies produced raw materials or agricultural products—was breached as handfuls of newly industrialized countries (NICs) began to emerge as significant exporters of manufactured goods into world markets.[25] In this situation, competition among producers of manufactured goods intensified dramatically, profit margins were squeezed, and pressures for cost-cutting or wholesale industrial restructuring became irresistible.

Employers began to abandon more rigid practices associated with Fordist mass production in favor of more flexible systems of "lean production" now associated with post-Fordist capitalism.[26] Central to these transformations was the drive to weaken the bargaining power of unionized labor and seek out "flexible" labor markets in which unionized workers would face competition from nonunion, lower-wage labor.[27] As a result of colonialism, which had economically as well as politically subordinated much of the non-European world, and pervasive systems of racial and gender discrimination, which have been operative worldwide, employers seeking more "flexible" labor arrangements had no difficulty finding large pools of unorganized, vulnerable, and therefore "cheap" labor, especially in the postcolonial world. As a result, developing countries have been increasingly, if unevenly, incorporated into global production networks. This globalization of production has substantially enhanced the powers of employers in relation to their workers. For workers in developed countries, globalization means that employers are able more credibly to threaten plant relocation and job loss when faced with collective bargaining situations, and there is strong evidence from the U.S. case to suggest that this is increasingly widespread.[28] Restructuring labor relations, along with the emergence of multinational firms and the transnational organization of production, have been crucial aspects of globalization.

Agnew and Corbridge explain that this is partly understandable in terms of the complex economic and political calculations of transnational corporations (TNCs):

> TNCs have been attracted to developing countries that are reasonably well managed and that show signs of economic growth and development. TNCs do not generally set up shop in countries like Bangladesh or Sudan, no matter how low unit labor costs might be in such countries. They prefer to locate in countries where labor is cheap by the standards of the high-income economies, but which is also skilled or semi-skilled and disciplined in the ways of the market and time-management.[29]

They summarize the implications of these developments in terms of the unfolding deterritorialization of economic activity: "[T]he internationalization of production capital has been significant for the way that it has helped to explode the unity so often assumed to exist between a given country's 'economic interests' and the interests of a particular territorial economy."[30] Thus, to take a famous example from American history, it is no longer necessarily the case that what is good for General Motors—or any other TNC—is good for America.

Dramatic reductions in transportation and communication costs combined with the breakdown of Fordist/Keynesian regimes in core countries have made it possible for firms to coordinate production on a truly global scale. Seeking to escape the profit squeeze of the end of the Fordist era, many multinational corporations (MNCs) embarked on a global production strategy. Whether automobiles, sneakers, or even services such as data entry or customer service, the production of goods and services is increasingly a global process. This trend is a dramatic example of the qualitatively different world the contemporary economy represents relative to the global economy of the turn of the nineteenth century, where the predominant pattern of trade involved the exchange of primary products (raw materials, minerals, and agricultural products) from the postcolonial world and finished manufactured goods from the industrial capitalist countries.

In contrast to the international trading patterns of a century ago, MNCs, transnational production, and intrafirm trade have emerged as important forms of global economic linkage in the contemporary world economy.[31] According to United Nations estimates reported by Held and his coauthors, "Sales of foreign affiliates [that is, overseas branches of MNCs] have grown faster than world exports: in the 1970s and 1980s they had achieved levels comparable with world export levels but in the late 1990s they were around 30 percent higher. Foreign affiliates' sales as a percentage of world GDP [i.e., global economic output] has risen from 10–15 percent in the 1970s to around 25 percent today."[32] Somewhere between one-quarter and one-third of world trade now consists of "intrafirm" trade—transactions among different branches of particular multinational firms. While the great bulk of multinational corporate activity remains concentrated in the most advanced capitalist countries, developing countries have been increasingly, if unevenly, incorporated into these global production networks.[33] As production has been rationalized on a transnational scale, the traditional global division of labor—in which manufacturing activities were concentrated in the advanced capitalist "core" areas while postcolonial "peripheral" areas were limited to primary production—has been breached and NICs have emerged as significant producers of manufactured goods for the world economy.[34] According to the World Bank, "in 1990, 17 percent of the labor force in developing and formerly centrally planned economies worked directly or indirectly in the export sector, with exports to the richer countries accounting for two-thirds of this employment effect. [Further,] . . . the share of manufactures in developing countries' exports tripled between 1970 and 1990, from 20 percent to 60 percent."[35]

The growing significance of transnational production chains and intra-industry trade can be seen by looking at the percentage of "import content" in finished manufactured goods. As firms have increasingly outsourced components of the production process, more and more of the inputs that go into finished manufactures are accounted for by "intermediate goods" produced in segments of the production chain located overseas, then imported into the country where they are incorporated into finished goods. Think about the computer on your desktop; it may have been assembled by a computer dealer in your country or even in your town, but the major

43

components (circuit boards, disk drives, etc.) that went into the computer case probably originated in Taiwan, Malaysia, Singapore, Hong Kong, China, Japan, or elsewhere in the global economy. It is this kind of *trade within the production chain*—which economists call "intra-industry" trade—that will be reflected in figures on the import content of manufactured goods. Such figures for eight major industrial countries between the years 1899 and 1985 are presented in table 2.1.

First, note that all countries in this table, with the exception of Japan, show a dramatic increase in the import content of manufactured goods over the century or so covered by these data. By the end of the century, all countries except Japan exhibited levels that were substantially higher than at the beginning—for the U.S., eight times higher. Note also that this growth was fastest in the late twentieth century, especially from 1971 to 1985. During this fourteen-year period the percentage for the U.S. more than doubled, rising from 9 to 24 percent. Measures such as these strongly suggest that production is an increasingly globalized phenomenon, and that the globalizing economy of recent decades is qualitatively different from the international economy of the late nineteenth century.

To summarize this part of our discussion, then, an important difference in the contemporary global economy, relative to the nineteenth-century era of free trade, is the increasing proliferation of globalized production chains. The ongoing globalization of production is politically consequential. It puts increasing pressure on what is left of the Fordist accommodation in the old industrial core of the world economy, insofar as the increasingly credible threat of capital flight, lost jobs, and tax revenues undermines the bargaining power of organized workers and discourages the

Table 2.1   Import Content of Finished Manufactures, 1899–1985 (Percent)

	1899	1913	1950	1963	1971	1985
United Kingdom	16	17	04	07	12	29
France	12	13	07	12	17	27
Germany	16	10	04	10	16	26
Italy	11	14	08	13	12	20
Sweden	08	14	12	17	37	46
United States	03	03	02	03	09	24
Canada	20	23	16	18	37	45
Japan	30	34	03	06	04	06

Source: David Held, A. McGrew, D. Goldblatt, and J. Perraton, *Global Transformations* (Cambridge: Polity, 1999), 174.

full-employment policies characteristic of Keynesianism. For workers in developing countries, globalization may imply opportunities for employment that might not otherwise be available, but along with employment come the subordination and exploitation entailed in the capitalist labor process.[36]

Debt Crisis and Globalization of Finance

The process of transnational industrial restructuring described above received further impetus from a massive debt crisis that seized many of the developing countries of the world during the last two decades of the twentieth century. Enormous changes had occurred in the world of international finance, unleashing forces that could easily destabilize the most vulnerable economies and threaten the stability of the world financial system itself. The story is long and complex, but we attempt to explain its most significant elements as straightforwardly as possible.

That aspect of the Bretton Woods regime that featured the U.S. dollar as the key currency for world trade, with its value backed by gold at a fixed exchange rate, had unraveled by the early 1970s. With its massive outflows of overseas investment and its global military presence, the U.S. had pumped dollars into the global economy for much of the postwar period, providing the "liquidity" needed for growing international trade and investment. By the 1970s, the financial cost of fighting a losing battle in Vietnam was approaching $150 billion or more. U.S. advantages in manufacturing and its surplus in merchandise trade were eroding. America's overall balance of payments deficit was becoming increasingly massive and more or less permanent, generating even more outflows of U.S. dollars into the world economy. Huge and rapidly growing stocks of U.S. dollars were accumulating overseas, continuously creating new potential claims on finite U.S. gold reserves. Under these circumstances, foreign holders of dollars began to doubt that the U.S. could continue to back the dollar with gold at the rate originally specified at Bretton Woods. This situation created a strong incentive for international dollar holders to redeem their dollars for gold *before* the U.S. could renege on its commitment. U.S. gold supplies dwindled as confidence in the dollar eroded: "By 1968, America's gold stock was half of what it had been in 1950."[37] President Nixon severed the dollar's officially guaranteed relationship to gold in 1971. Following the demise of the Bretton Woods "fixed" exchange rate system, a system of "floating" exchange rates emerged in which the value of the dollar in relation to other currencies would fluctuate in response to global supply and demand for those particular currencies.

As dollars poured out of the U.S., substantial quantities of internationally held dollars were deposited in overseas bank accounts outside the regulatory control of the U.S. government and became known as "Eurodollars." The collapse of the Bretton Woods fixed-rate regime and its associated capital controls coincided with the emergence of Eurodollars and other unregulated, effectively deterritorialized currencies, and together these developments resulted in breathtaking volumes of foreign exchange trading and speculative international investment (in which speculators place enormous bets on short-term fluctuations of international currency values). Foreign exchange trading now dwarfs the currency reserves of governments and can readily swamp, or leave high and dry, the financial markets of particular nations.[38] Responding to short-term differences in perceived conditions of profitability and variations in business confidence between one place and another, as well as speculative guesses about future market fluctuations, these enormous flows are highly volatile. Vast sums can be shifted from one currency (or assets denominated in one currency) to another almost at the speed of light via the computer modems and fiber-optic cables that link together the world's financial markets and enable round-the-clock trading.

It is against this backdrop of global "hot money" that we must view the debt crisis that engulfed most of the developing world in the last two decades of the twentieth century. In a world awash in cash (especially dollars) seeking profitable investment, there was a surge of aggressive private bank lending to developing countries beginning in the 1970s. The Organization of Petroleum Exporting Countries (OPEC) engineered a fourfold increase in the world market price of oil beginning in 1973, resulting in vast new deposits of dollars in the bank accounts of oil exporting countries and contributing mightily to the easy-money binge of international private bank lending during that decade. By the end of the decade, a house of cards had been constructed in the global financial system, shakily standing atop "about $350 billions of OPEC surpluses; almost $400 billions of Third World debt; and a quadrupling of unregulated Eurodollars to $425 billion."[39]

The proximate cause of the global debt crisis was a major shift in U.S. economic policy begun in 1979. Motivated by the desire to restrain inflation (that is, generally rising prices across the economy as a whole) and to prevent a massive sell-off of U.S. dollars in foreign exchange markets and a consequent collapse in the value of the dollar, the Federal Reserve instituted a drastic tightening of monetary policy in the U.S. Interest rates rose sharply, and overall economic activity declined. Since borrowing for both investment and consumption became more expensive at the higher prevailing interest rates, the U.S. and countries economically interdependent with it fell into recession. The effect on indebted developing countries was catastrophic, as Walden Bello explains: "[E]ach percentage point increase in international interest rates added hundreds of millions of dollars to the yearly debt service of countries which had agreed to loans set not at fixed but at variable interest rates."[40] Heavily indebted developing countries were caught in a vise: They faced much higher debt service payments even as their export revenues declined due to the recession in the world economy. One after another, developing countries hit the wall, unable to pay their existing debt obligations.

As lender of last resort, the IMF was the global institution to which many indebted countries turned for help with their financial crises. The IMF (and perhaps to a lesser degree its sister institution, the World Bank) was governed by an ideology that has become known as "neoliberalism" or "the Washington Consensus"—strongly favored by the predominant actor in these global financial institutions, the U.S. Treasury Department. Overlooking systemic problems such as global hot money or the perverse role of the dollar in global financial markets, the Washington Consensus instead located the primary cause of the debt crisis in the inability of poor countries to live within their means, restrain consumption, encourage investment, and repay their debts. Corresponding to this diagnosis, neoliberalism prescribed a combination of strict market discipline and openness to international trade and investment, a combination that became known as "structural adjustment." At the heart of structural adjustment is an imposed austerity that ratchets downward real material standards of living in order to reduce consumption and cheapen labor, attract foreign investors, and enable the indebted country to earn the foreign exchange required to pay its creditors. IMF loans then became conditional upon a country's compliance with structural adjustment programs. Walden Bello summarizes the global political economy of austerity that emerged in the 1980s thus: "with over 70 Third World countries submitting to IMF and World Bank programs in the 1980s, stabilization, structural adjustment, and shock therapy became the common condition of the [global] South in that decade."[41]

While IMF intervention is a welcome relief for international investors, for the people of the indebted country this is bitter medicine indeed, as economist Robin Hahnel explains:

> IMF policy is not designed to help the majority in troubled economies. It is intended to help international creditors in the short run, and increase returns on global capital in the long run. . . . [International creditors']

47

chances of getting repaid are better the higher the value of the local currency of their borrowers, since profits in that currency must be turned into dollars to repay them. Their chances of being repaid are better the larger the surplus of exports over imports, since that is one source of dollars to repay them. . . . So anything that props up exchange rates or boosts exports and lowers imports is in the interest of international creditors. . . . High local interest rates attract international capital in the short run, which increases demand for the local currency and boosts its value. Lower levels of production mean lower incomes, lower demand for imports, larger trade surpluses, and therefore also upward pressure on the value of the local currency. Expanding the trade surplus and propping up the local currency are the only ways local debtors can pay off their international creditors quickly, and that is why they are the key to every component of IMF stabilization policy. . . . The deflationary monetary and fiscal policies used to stabilize the currency and reduce imports bring a halt to productive investment, growth and development, and throw the local economy into recession or worse, with dramatic drops in production, income, and employment. But the disastrous effects on the local economy are irrelevant to those who impose the policy, because protecting the local currency and expanding the trade surplus are necessary if international creditors are to be repaid.[42]

These developments have been profoundly significant, for the emerging historical structures of neoliberal capitalism embody an enhancement of the social powers of capital, especially finance capital, which can discourage or deter Keynesian-inspired macroeconomic policies aimed at increasing employment or wage levels. Accordingly, the globalization of finance has been accompanied by a resurgence of laissez-faire fundamentalism since the late 1970s, as neoliberal austerity has largely eclipsed the growth-oriented ideology that originally underpinned the postwar world economy. This disciplinary power has the effect of prioritizing the interests of investors, who are as a class effectively able to hold entire states or societies hostage. The particular interests of the owning class are represented as if they were the general interests of all: "[S]ince profit is the necessary condition of universal expansion, capitalists appear within capitalist societies as bearers of a universal interest."[43] In this ideological construction, the social and moral claims of working people and the poor are reduced to the pleadings of "special interests," which must be resisted in order to secure the conditions of stable accumulation. In William Greider's apt summary: "Like bondholders in general, the new governing consensus explicitly assumed that faster economic growth was dangerous—threatening to the stable financial order—so nations were effectively blocked from measures that might reduce permanent unemployment or ameliorate the decline in wages. . . . Governments were expected to withdraw more and more benefits from dependent classes of citizens—the poor and elderly and unemployed—but also in various ways from the broad middle class, in order to honor their obligations to the creditor class."[44] To the extent that state managers understand the world in terms of ideologies of hyperglobalization, this very real disciplinary power is intensified to the point that consideration of pro-worker or environmentally friendly policies is precluded, and policies may be specifically designed to attract and hold (putatively footloose) capital by offering the most favorable business climate possible. Indeed, as we saw above, this is a central part of the ideological justification for the package of austerity policies that the IMF typically imposes on developing countries experiencing financial crisis—the latter itself being largely a result of systemic forces, especially the globalization of finance and its attendant exchange rate instabilities.

To summarize this part of the discussion, then, we may say that neoliberal policy prescriptions have entailed an enforced emphasis on "free" markets; a private sector unencumbered by public concerns or government regulation; increased global openness to flow of goods, services, and capital to maximize profit opportunities; strict limits on fiscal and monetary policies (i.e., anti-Keynesian) and slower growth to prevent inflation and limit bargaining power of labor; austerity as the fundamental response to debt; and lower real standards of living to enable repayment of bankers and investors. The result of a global order of austerity has been redistribution of wealth and social power away from working people and toward investors and employers and greater inequality within and between rich and poor countries.

The modern world has become increasingly unequal over the last two centuries, with this inequality becoming much more (rather than less) marked as globalization has accelerated under U.S. leadership in recent decades. Table 2.2 suggests that, as a historical process, globalization has produced an increasingly hierarchical world of structured inequality.

Table 2.2   The Modern World Is Increasingly Unequal: Income Ratio of World's Richest 20 Percent of Countries to Poorest 20 Percent of Countries

1820	1870	1913	1960	1990	1997
3:1	7:1	11:1	30:1	60:1	74:1

Source: United Nations, *Human Development Report 1999* (Oxford: Oxford University Press, 1999), 3.

By the close of the twentieth century, the richest fifth of the world's countries was earning income *seventy four times* as much as the poorest fifth. According to the UN's *Human Development Report* for 2002, "The level of inequality worldwide is grotesque":

- "The world's richest 1% of people receive as much income as the poorest 57%."
- "The income of the world's richest 5% is 114 times that of the poorest 5%."
- "The richest 10% of the U.S. population has an income equal to that of the poorest 43% of the world. Put differently, the income of the richest 25 million Americans is equal to that of almost 2 billion people."[45]

While growing global inequality is difficult to deny, the evidence concerning globalization and poverty is rather more ambiguous. According to the World Bank, during the decade between 1987 and 1998, the proportion of the population in developing and postcommunist countries who live on income less than one dollar per day (the World Bank standard of income poverty) decreased significantly, from 28 percent to 24 percent. At the same time, due to population growth, the absolute number of people living at this level of poverty has increased slightly and now represents 1.2 billion people.[46] In light of rapid globalization, exploding inequality, and stubborn poverty, even some highly placed insiders have come to question the governing ideology of the global economy.

An Insider's Critique of Neoliberal Orthodoxy

A distinguished academic economist drawn into important policy roles—former chairman of the U.S. President's Council of Economic Advisors, former chief economist at the World Bank, and Nobel Prize laureate—Joseph Stiglitz has had firsthand experience inside the governing institutions of neoliberal globalization. He shares with the mainstream of his profession a general presumption in favor of markets as the institutional form that will tend to maximize choice, efficiency, prosperity, and freedom. However, Stiglitz rejects what he calls the "market fundamentalism" that for decades has been the governing ideology of the IMF, authorizing the imposition of austerity, privatization, and market liberalization on scores of developing countries facing chronic indebtedness and recurrent balance of payments crises.[47] Contrary to neoliberalism's dogmatic insistence on the prioritization of markets, Stiglitz leans toward a view of the economy as embedded within larger sets of social institutions. If those institutions are not deliberately arranged so as to support more sustainable, equitable economic growth, liberalization of trade or finance will not by itself produce these outcomes.[48] Insofar as the IMF's exercise of compulsory power over indebted developing countries has proscribed state action to secure these preconditions—even as it imposed austerity, privatization, and liberalization—the results have been unnecessary economic contraction and social dislocation, compound opportunity costs of lost economic growth, impoverishment and deepening inequality, economic instability, and political backlash. Stiglitz fears that these perverse outcomes may imperil the broader economic and social gains that he believes globalization could bring, if properly managed. While the original, Keynesian orientation of the Bretton Woods institutions might have been open to securing the social preconditions for "globalization with a human face," Stiglitz believes that the Washington Consensus, which has been entrenched most firmly at the IMF since the Reagan–Thatcher era, is ultimately self-defeating.[49]

To account for this perverse system and its governing ideology, Stiglitz looks toward the political relations and social powers at work in the global economy: "The [global economic] institutions are dominated not just by the wealthiest industrial countries but by commercial and financial interests in those countries, and the policies of the institutions naturally reflect this."[50] The problem appears to be rooted in a contradiction—institutionalized disavowal of the implicitly public, political character of these institutions and their activities and a concomitant lack of public accountability or participation:

> There was a certain irony in the stance of the IMF. It tried to pretend that it was above politics, yet it was clear that its lending program was, in part, driven by politics. . . . The IMF is a public institution, established with money provided by taxpayers around the world. This is important to remember because it does not report directly to either the citizens who finance it or those whose lives it affects. Rather, it reports to the ministries of finance and the central banks of the governments of the world.[51]

These latter institutions, in turn, "are closely tied to the financial community," their officials often drawn from banks or financial firms to which they will return upon completing their term of public service. By virtue of these ties, "the IMF was . . . reflecting the interests and ideology of the western financial community," upholding the sanctity of private property and contract, and striking preemptively at perceived inflationary tendencies that might erode the real value of creditors' assets. Instead of approaching development as a broad-based "transformation of society," IMF policies became focused on "protecting investors."[52] Despite the political character and public consequences of what they are and what they do, the institutions of global economic governance are not directly accountable to the public but are politically and ideologically predisposed toward bankers and investors from the major capitalist countries. Stiglitz boldly concludes that the institutions of global governance are "antidemocratic," "a disenfranchisement" of people worldwide, in effect a "new dictatorship of international finance."[53] These are strong words indeed, and all the more so coming as they do from a market-oriented economist and experienced policy advisor.

Conclusion: Neoliberalism and Politics

It is deeply ironic that neoliberalism's resurrection of market fundamentalism has been attendant upon the increasing extensity and intensity of transnational relations. Even as people in locations around the globe are increasingly integrated into transnational social relations, neoliberalism seeks to remove these relations from the public sphere—where they might be subjected to norms of democratic governance—and instead subject them to the power of capital as expressed through the discipline of the market. In general, the neoliberal agenda of integrating and depoliticizing the global economy fosters a "race to the bottom," which enhances capitalist power through intensified market competition and the dull compulsion of economic relations. Such an implicit class bias is evident in the WTO's governance of the global trading system. The WTO has refused to link human rights or labor rights protections to participation in the global trading system; its rules forbid discrimination against traded goods based on how they were produced—outwardly similar goods must be treated similarly regardless of whether they were produced by processes abusive to workers or environment—and the WTO's trade-related investment measures (TRIMs) proscribe performance requirements placed on foreign investment and shield MNCs from potentially important kinds of host government regulation, such as those requiring linkages with local economies, and thus higher levels of employment, developmental spinoffs, etc.[54] Taken together, these aspects of WTO governance promote nodes of uneven development linked into globalizing production systems. And, in combination with the draconian austerity programs, public sector retrenchment, openness to foreign investment, and export orientation enforced by the IMF upon many of the world's developing countries, all of this facilitates capital's intensified exploitation of labor and environment through transnational production and commodity chains.

It is important analytically and politically to note that the world of cheap labor in which transnational production is organized is a world that is neither race nor gender neutral. The great bulk of workers in export processing zones (EPZs)—the most labor-intensive nodes of global production chains—are young women.[55] Their labor may be culturally constructed as cheap insofar as they are presumed to be under the social umbrella of a male (either father or husband) and therefore not requiring a self-sufficiency wage, and insofar as the gender division of labor marks off "women's work" as "something that girls and women do 'naturally' or 'traditionally'" rather than the expression of hard-won, and more highly rewarded, skill—this latter presumptively an attribute of more masculine employments.[56] Further, the austerity programs of neoliberalism heavily affect women, intensifying the double burden of gendered work as retrenchment of public services puts greater burdens on households—and therefore feminized domestic labor—for the care of children, the elderly, the sick—even as those same cutbacks affect areas of the gender division of labor, such as education and health care, in which women are concentrated.[57] Economic austerity and a narrowing of options may then channel women toward employment in export industries and EPZs, or into the informal sector. Moreover, Eurocentrism and racism have generated representations of naturalized poverty among peoples of color in the developing world, attributed to a lack of those things that are presumed to distinguish the more developed (and white) countries—capital, technology, managerial expertise, effective and honest governance, skilled labor, and so forth.[58] Liberalization of, trade with, and investment in the developing world may then appear as the twenty-first-century version of the "white man's burden." Bound up with capitalist globalization, then, are ideologies and relations of gender- and race-based domination. Capitalism may not have created these dominance relations, but it has effectively internalized them within the historical structures of capitalist globalization.

NEW FORMS OF GLOBAL POWER
AND RESISTANCE

Important as they have been, the globalizations of production, investment, and finance, and the growing powers of formal global institutions such as the IMF and the WTO, do not comprise the whole story of global political economy. Globalization has also involved the development of new modes of transnational politics, new forms of power and resistance emerging in civil society, among NGOs, and through transnational social movements. In this chapter and the next, we bring into the foreground of discussion some of these new forms of politics and assess their significance for the production of alternative possible worlds.

Among the most important insights of Marxian theory is that the seemingly apolitical economic spaces generated by capitalism—within and across nation-states—are permeated by structured relations of social power deeply consequential for social life as a whole. One of the most important, if also most neglected, aspects of capitalism is the way in which its core structures of private property generate tremendous social powers, which are privately held and exercised in the interest of private profit (recall our discussions in chapters 1 and 2). These powers may be ideologically depoliticized—and thus rendered democratically unaccountable—in liberal ideologies that presuppose the separation of a naturalized and privatized economy from the explicitly political sphere of the state (e.g., John Locke's theory of property acquired in the "state of nature," or Adam Smith's account of the spontaneous emergence of division of labor and market exchange among rationally self-interested individuals). Once this ideological separation has been accomplished, the operation of this privatized economy (and the implicit social powers residing within it) may then be represented as something approaching a universal social good, the engine of economic growth and a generalized prosperity (as in Adam Smith's famous "invisible hand," which leads self-interested individuals to produce socially useful goods and services in the most efficient possible way). Obscuring from view the relations of social power at work within the economy, prevailing liberal ideologies present the economy as an apolitical space in which individual consumers make choices about which commodities best satisfy their needs and wants, and private producers compete to satisfy the demands of consumers.

But the fact that these power relations are well disguised by liberal ideologies does not mean that they are invulnerable, for another of the basic Marxian insights on which we draw is that social power relations are also *processes*—in no way automatic or necessarily self-sustaining, indeed fraught with tension and possibilities for conflict and change. Social power relations are always to some extent reciprocal, a two-way street; they are continually reenacted and depend upon the ongoing participation of both dominant and subordinate parties. They may then be likened to a dance in which each participant has a necessary role within the context of the performance and hence some (although not necessarily equal or symmetrical) power to shape the performance as a whole. Accordingly, we understand the politics of globalization in terms of a *dialectic of power* subject to ongoing contestation, renegotiation, and restructuring. The reproduction of these powers is hardly assured and must be politically secured on a continuing basis. In other words, the apparent "truth" of liberal ideologies positing an apolitical economy is being continually called into question by the (re)eruption of more or less explicitly political struggles surrounding the very relations of economic power that liberalism pretends do not exist.

Viewed in this way, the structures of globalizing capitalism generate not only possibilities for domination and exploitation, but also new forms of potential solidarity in resistance to these. People engaged in such struggles may come to understand themselves as collective political actors, working together toward convergent (if not congruent) visions of alternative possible worlds, rather than as individual consumers pursuing satisfaction through acquisition of commodities or private producers seeking profits. Such forms of solidarity have in recent decades taken on an increasingly transnational character. In this chapter and the next we see that battles over globalization may be understood in terms of such a dialectic of power, involving the construction and contestation of new forms of social power on a global scale. Sometimes these dances of power and resistance have centered more explicitly on relations of class, while at other times gender and nationality or race have been highly significant; it is important to keep in mind, however, that these forms of social power are often interwoven in complex ways.

A Global Hegemonic Project? The World Economic Forum

Globalization encompasses a variety of political and cultural relationships that are not reducible to economics, but it has been, and continues to be, bound up with the structures and dynamics of capitalism. As discussed in the preceding chapter, globalization has never been alien to capitalism, which—as a system of social relations premised upon the relentless drive for limitless accumulation—cannot rest content contained within territorial or other social boundaries. Yet capitalist globalization has in recent decades become more rapid, intense, and extensive than ever before. The acceleration of globalization in the late twentieth century was intimately involved with restructuring of capitalist institutions in response to the crisis of profitability that gripped Fordist-Keynesian capitalism. As part of these processes of restructuring, internationally active segments of the capitalist class have organized to frame common interests, to project a universalizing worldview that effectively depoliticizes the economic sphere (the ideology of neoliberalism), and to coordinate their own political action to realize their interests and visions. The kind of capitalist globalization we observe in recent decades has been the political project of a tendentially transnational—if also U.S.-led—historic bloc comprising globally oriented fractions of the capitalist class, state managers and international bureaucrats, journalists, and intellectuals. One important vehicle for these processes of strategizing, coordinating, and projecting a coherent ideological vision for globalizing capitalism has been the World Economic Forum (WEF).

Evolving out of the European Management Forum, which Swiss business professor Klaus Schwab founded in 1971, the WEF has become a membership organization for over 1,000 major international firms, each of which pays substantial annual fees to the Forum. The Forum explains in its promotional literature why shrewd businesspeople see this as money well spent: "As a member of the World Economic Forum, you are part of a real Club, and the foremost business and public-interest network in the world." In keeping with its motto of promoting "entrepreneurship in the public interest," the WEF brings its members together at an annual extravaganza in the ritzy Swiss ski resort of Davos. The Davos meetings offer WEF members "intensive networking in a privileged context allowing for the identification of new business opportunities and new business trends." At Davos, WEF members hobnob with their fellow global capitalists but also with leaders from political and civil society to whom the Forum refers as "constituents" to distinguish them from WEF "members"; while paying corporate "members" are entitled to attend WEF events, "constituents"— heads of state and government ministers, academics and policy experts, media figures and cultural leaders from around the world—may attend by invitation only. Thus, the WEF offers its members privileged access to "high-level interaction between political leaders and business leaders on the key issues affecting economic development" on regional and global scales.[1]

> The key to Forum activities is direct access to strategic decision-makers, in a framework designed to encourage economic development via private sector involvement. This direct interaction between public and private sector and experts leads to the creation of a partnership committed to improving the state of the world.[2]

According to Charles McLean, the WEF's director of communications, the Forum represents "a global town hall of leaders from different segments of society."

> For more than 30 years the World Economic Forum has brought together the major stakeholders in society—business leaders, government leaders, academics, journalists, writers, artists, religious leaders and representatives of civil society—to tackle humanity's biggest challenges.[3]

Manifesting in classic form the contradictory nature of capitalist power—simultaneously *private* and *social*—the WEF represents itself as being at once a private club and a kind of global public sphere. The Forum is an organization in which the various segments of the global power bloc can come together under the leadership of transnational capital to construct a unifying political vision and present to the rest of the world the interests of global capital in the guise of a universal vision—"entrepreneurship in the public interest." In short, it attempts to organize the hegemony of a global ruling class, as Kees van der Pijl has argued.[4]

And business has been booming for the brokers of the global "public sphere": In 2002 each of the one thousand WEF members paid an annual membership fee of $17,647 and an additional $7,353 per attendee for the privilege of sending their executives to the Davos meeting.[5] A smaller group of member firms pay very substantial additional sums to the Forum for the influence and prestige of being designated "partners." In 2000, at least twenty-seven major firms paid an additional quarter million dollars each for the privilege of being "knowledge partners" or "institutional partners." Two dozen others paid $78,000 to become "annual meeting partners." According to its web page, in 2002 the WEF had thirty-six corporate "strategic partners" and thirty "annual meeting partners." Partners enjoy a leading role in planning the Davos extravaganza and, not surprisingly, are highly visible participants: "They buy sessions," one former WEF staffer told the *Washington Post*.[6] "Entrepreneurship in the public interest" has been a hot commodity:

> Being the foremost organization promoting corporate-driven globalization has been very lucrative for the WEF. Since the World Trade Organization went into effect in 1995, WEF income grew by 148%, from $42 million in 1995 to $104 million in 2001. WEF member fees have grown nearly as quickly, rising 121% between 1995 and 2001, from $17 million to $38 million.[7]

While claiming to speak for the global public good, the WEF in fact primarily serves the interests of its paying members—the elite of transnational corporate capital. But the WEF is unrepresentative in other ways as well. A new report from Public Citizen/Global Trade Watch makes it clear that North American and European participants (including members and invited guests) dominate the WEF annual meeting. Further, members of the WEF governing boards are "overwhelmingly male, predominantly white and substantially from the wealthiest nations of Europe, North America and Japan."[8] At the pinnacle of global economic power, relations of race- and gender-based privilege are very much in evidence.

In recent years the WEF has become increasingly preoccupied with the contentious politics of neoliberal globalization. At the 1996 Davos conclave—well before the 1999 Seattle demonstrations brought widespread attention to the explosive potential of these issues—the Forum's central theme was "sustaining globalization." Forum organizers Klaus Schwab and Claude Smadja suggested that the process of globalization "has entered a critical phase" in which economic and political relationships, both globally and within countries, are being painfully restructured. They acknowledged that these changes are having a devastating impact on large numbers of working people in "the industrial democracies," with heightened mass insecurity resulting in "the rise of a new brand of populist politicians"—the likes of Patrick Buchanan in the U.S., Jean-Marie Le Pen of France, the Austrian politician Jörg Haider, and others who base their political appeal on claiming to speak for "the people" of their nations as opposed to self-serving transnational "elites." WEF leaders feared that in the absence of effective measures to address the difficult circumstances of working people and the weakened ideological legitimacy of global capitalism, the new populisms might continue to gain strength, threaten further progress toward the agenda of globalization, and "test the social fabric of the democracies in an unprecedented way." The social forces leading globalization, then, face "the challenge of demonstrating how the new global capitalism can function to the benefit of the majority and not only for corporate managers and investors."[9] In the spirit of this analysis, Schwab addressed the opening session of the 1996 forum: "Business has become a major stakeholder of globalization and has a direct responsibility to contribute to the stability of our global system."[10]

This theme of global capitalists managing the politics of capitalist globalization has continued to hold a special place in the WEF's long-term agenda. Almost a year prior to Seattle, a preemptive vision of "globalization with a human face" was being explicitly constructed as a central theme of the 1999 Davos Forum. Schwab and Smadja struck a note of urgency:

> We are confronted with what is becoming an explosive contradiction. At a time when the emphasis is on empowering people, on democracy moving ahead all over the world, on people asserting control over their own lives, globalization has established the supremacy of the market in an unprecedented way. . . . We must demonstrate that globalization is not just a code word for an exclusive focus on shareholder value at the expense of any other consideration; that the free flow of goods and capital does not develop to the detriment of the most vulnerable segments of the population and of some accepted social and human standards. . . . If we do not invent ways to make globalization more inclusive, we have to face the prospect of a resurgence of the acute social confrontations of the past, magnified at the international level.[11]

As interesting as the acuity of the WEF's diagnosis, however, was the infirmity of its prescribed treatment. In his opening address, Schwab exhorted members of the global power bloc to "try to define a responsible globality" based on an ethic of "caring for the neighbors in our global village."[12] The transnational power of corporate capital would not be compromised; rather, they would ponder the possibility of ruling in a more beneficent fashion to legitimize and sustain that power. Such calls for corporate civic leadership have been reiterated in subsequent years.

In order to maintain the barest credibility of its rhetorical stance of inclusive and open dialogue in the face of burgeoning protest movements and increasingly assertive and well-informed critics, with much fanfare and self-congratulation the WEF invited a number of critical individuals and NGOs to participate in its annual meeting in 2001. When Swiss authorities cracked down harshly on demonstrators attempting to reach Davos to voice their criticisms outside the WEF, some of the invited guests inside were unmannered enough to complain to the Swiss government and WEF leadership. "NGOs acting like NGOs and demanding civil liberties and basic democratic rights were not favorably received."[13] Confronted by the criticisms of invited guests—who argued that the exclusivity of "fortress Davos" was the underlying cause of the violence and that the WEF should open itself to civil society groups—WEF managing director Claude Smadja tellingly responded: "We invite whoever we believe is relevant to open dialogue. We are not the United Nations. We are a private organization."[14] The experiment, it seems, was not judged to have been a success, and such leading lights of the global justice movement as Martin Khor of Third World Network, Walden Bello of Focus on the Global South, representatives of Public Citizen, and others were not invited to return the following year. The *Financial Times* reported: "The Forum says it is not inviting organizations that contribute only negative views and do not support its 'mission' to narrow global divisions."[15]

While the Forum claims "a long-standing policy of inclusion when it comes to non-governmental organizations and representatives of civil society," Public Citizen estimates that such groups typically account for less than 2 percent of attendees at the annual WEF extravaganza.[16] A few less militant or confrontational critics may still be included in WEF deliberations (prominent in 2002 was rock star Bono), but most are relegated to the heavily guarded sidewalks outside or to alternative venues such as the World Social Forum in Porto Alegre, Brazil. Meanwhile, the WEF has not renounced its larger hegemonic project of "globalization with a human face" and indeed has now repackaged its brand of public-spirited but privately managed capitalism as a solution to global terrorism. In general, the WEF continues to seek ways to soften the hard edge of global capitalism and to present globalization as a process that is generally beneficial to humankind even as it sustains and strengthens the private powers of global capital.

Alternative Visions: Globalization from Below

Over the last several years, a variety of social movements and activist-oriented NGOs have coalesced into what has become widely (if inaccurately) known as the "antiglobalization movement." A kind of coalition of coalitions, the movement for global justice is a constellation of sometimes convergent, sometimes parallel, and sometimes divergent social forces that share a common hostility, not to globalization as such but to *capitalist* globalization and its neoliberal institutions.

Reverberating throughout the movement for global justice is the influence of the Zapatistas of Chiapas. Synthesizing Western radical philosophy and cosmologies of North American indigenous peoples into a syncretic political vision,[17] Subcommandante Marcos (Zapatista leader and theorist) clearly links the Zapatista struggle against neoliberalism—inaugurated on the very day NAFTA went into effect (January 1, 1994)—to the 500-year-long history of European colonialism and North American imperialism: "Re-named as 'Neoliberalism' the historic crime in the concentration of privileges, wealth and impunities, democratizes misery and hopelessness."[18] The Zapatistas denounce neoliberalism as the vehicle for capitalism's commodification of social life: that is, turning ever-increasing parts of our lives into commodities to be bought and sold, and therefore subject to the compulsions of market competition in which "inefficient" and "unprofitable" activities are driven out of existence. The Zapatistas fear that imposition of a universal model of market-based development will result in "cultural assimilation and economic annihilation" of alternative ways of life—including their own.[19] Survival of the indigenous communities of Chiapas is understood to depend on struggles at multiple levels: "A world system makes it possible to transform crime into government in Mexico. A national system makes it possible for crime to rule in Chiapas. In the mountains of the Mexican Southeast, we struggle for our country, for humanity, and against neoliberalism."[20] Forging political connections between centuries-old anti-indigenous racism, the corrupt Mexican state, and global neoliberalism, Marcos and the Zapatistas effectively link the identities of indigenous peoples, Mexican peasants, members of civil society, and global resistors. With great effect, they reach out in solidarity to various persons and communities who felt their distinctive economic and cultural existences to be threatened by neoliberal capitalism: "[W]e are all the same because we are different," Marcos famously declared in an expression of solidarity with all who are marginalized.[21] Marcos and the Zapatistas imagine a world in which social difference would not automatically be interpreted in terms of superiority and inferiority, a world of dialogue and mutual respect across social and cultural differences, a world whose inhabitants "know themselves equal and different" and who therefore recognize "the possibility and necessity of speaking and listening," realizing "a world made of many worlds."[22] In such a world, democratic communities would govern themselves through inclusive dialogue, and their leaders would be responsible for realizing the community's wishes as expressed in the dialogue—that is, leaders would "rule by obeying."[23] Eschewing the conquest of state power (which would not effectively democratize Mexican or global society), the Zapatistas practice a complex multilevel politics that involves organizing self-determining base communities, resisting the military and ideological power of the Mexican state, coordinating with social movements and civil society groups across Mexico, and transnational networking among autonomous but related nodes of resistance. In Marcos's words, "We are the network, all of us who speak and listen. . . . We are the network, all of us who resist. . . . This intercontinental network of resistance, recognizing differences and acknowledging similarities, will strive to find itself in other resistances around the world."[24] And so it has.

The emergent Movement for Global Justice is complex and multifarious, aptly characterized as "a movement of movements," but there are significant commonalities on the basis of which we may describe these movements as forming a sort of confluence. Highlighting the most important factor bringing these various movements and agendas into (at least partial) alignment, Michael Hardt and Antonio Negri wrote:

> The protests themselves have become global movements, and one of their clearest objectives is the democratization of globalizing processes. This should not be called an anti-globalization movement. It is pro-globalization, or rather, it is an alternative globalization movement—one that seeks to eliminate inequalities between rich and poor and between the powerful and the powerless, and to expand the possibilities of self-determination.[25]

Expressing precisely this democratizing impulse, one street protester told the *New York Times* (February 3, 2002): "There's no magic solution, but we have to struggle and build a more democratic world from the ground up." Dan LaBotz—longtime labor activist now working with Global Exchange—casts the struggle explicitly in terms of democratic socialism:

> We need to construct a kind of socialism where workers, consumers, and ordinary citizens make the decisions through both direct and indirect democratic processes at all levels. . . . The most important thing is our long-range goal, ending corporate control of the economy and political life, and its replacement by a democratic popular power that can protect the planet, ensure human rights, and raise the standard of living in a new world of freedom and peace.[26]

Influential Canadian author-activist Naomi Klein suggests that the movement coalesces around "a radical reclaiming of the commons"—slowing, halting, or reversing tendencies toward privatization and commodification, which effectively colonize and consume public space, thereby displacing grassroots processes of democratic deliberation. "There is an emerging consensus," she writes, "that building community-based decision-making power—whether through unions, neighborhoods, farms, villages, anarchist collectives or aboriginal self-government—is essential to countering the might of multinational corporations."[27] This common thread, woven through what they call the "New Democracy Movement," is underscored by longtime author-activists Maude Barlow and Tony Clarke: "[T]he most persistent theme underlying the mobilization of popular resistance to corporate globalization is opposition to the systematic assault on democracy and the commons," which they name as "a form of global class warfare." "Developing a new democracy along these lines at local, national and international levels is the only possible antidote to corporate globalization."[28] On the broad terrain of formulations such as these—all of which presuppose a view of the world economy as a sphere of social power relations that can and should be reconstructed in more democratic, pluralistic, and enabling forms—community activists, indigenous peoples' groups, peasants and landless laborers, feminists, progressive unionists, anarchists, socialists, and autonomist radicals, as well as a plethora of other social forces, have found sufficient common ground to converge for collective acts of resistance in an impressive series of transnational protests that rocked the world.

But this convergence in opposition to neoliberal globalization does not imply unity. Within the movement there are sharp differences about strategy and tactics. At the broadest level of strategy, disagreements center on reforming, reconstructing, or abolishing global economic institutions in the course of constructing future possible worlds. The movement may be understood as having two broad wings in an uneasy alliance: One wing emphasizes institutional reform in order to limit the global race to the bottom and make global economic institutions (such as the WTO and IMF) and actors (such as international investors or multinational firms) publicly accountable and socially responsible; the other wing—inspired by anarchist traditions of political thought and practice—emphasizes the construction of new social institutions from the ground up, based on nonhierarchical voluntary associations and grassroots participatory democracy.

Global Networks of Resistance

Often thought of as a nineteenth-century political philosophy, anarchism has reemerged as an important form of political thought and practice on a global scale, animating various sectors of resistance to neoliberal globalization. Its influence is evident in the network-style organizational forms of global resistance; in tactics of direct action in opposition to hierarchic structures of inequality and oppression; and in its strategic emphasis on political practices that promote mutual cooperation, voluntary association, and grassroots democracy.

Anarchist traditions are diverse and, in some respects, divergent. Although anarchism as a whole defies straightforward summary, some major streams of anarchist thinking can be identified. Rudolf Rocker summarized the political horizon of social anarchism in the following terms:

> For the anarchist, freedom is not an abstract philosophical concept, but the vital concrete possibility for every human being to bring to full development all the powers, capacities, and talents which nature has endowed him with, and turn them to social account. . . . [T]he problem that is set for our time is that of freeing man from the curse of economic exploitation and political and social enslavement.[29]

The French philosopher and journalist Pierre-Joseph Proudhon (1809–1865) laid the intellectual groundwork for the social anarchist tradition. Since that time, anarchists have argued that the form of social organization most consistent with human freedom, mutual cooperation, and self-development is the directly self-governing voluntary association. Such associations, in turn, may join into federations or networks of associations, but these larger groupings must respect and facilitate the autonomy of affiliated associations if they are to avoid degenerating into an implicitly tyrannical hierarchy.

Between social anarchists and their communitarian political ideal stands the modern state with its formidable coercive apparatus. According to one strong current within the anarchist tradition, this state power is directly related to capitalist economic power. Anarchist-socialists in the tradition of Mikhail Bakunin (1814–1876) and Peter Kropotkin (1842–1921) have understood the state and capitalism as interdependent aspects of a system of domination. In this view, the coercive power of the state is deployed for the protection of private property and the defense of capitalist domination. Anarchists have portrayed parliamentary democracy as little more than a facade that masks these relations of domination. Accordingly, the state and capitalism have been objects of anarchist activity aimed at the realization of freedom through struggle against institutionalized oppression.

Among the leading contemporary thinkers in this tradition is Murray Bookchin, whose writings have infused social anarchism with a profound ecological sensibility. In contrast to traditional Marxist visions of a revolutionary proletariat led by a disciplined political party, Bookchin sees social hierarchy and exploitation to lie at the root of ecological crisis and envisions social change as emerging out of nonhierarchical voluntary associations representing a broad cross-section of society rather than a particular social class. Organized through voluntary affinity groups, Bookchin's archetypal anarchist revolutionary

> begins to challenge not only the economic and political premises of hierarchy, but hierarchy as such. He [sic] not only raises the need for social revolution but tries to *live* in a revolutionary manner to the degree that this is possible in the existing society. He not only attacks the forms created by the legacy of domination but also improvises new forms of liberation that take their poetry from the future.[30]

Bookchin's eco-anarchism has been profoundly influential among activists who oppose neoliberal globalization for its exploitation and degradation of the earth's natural environment.

Contemporary anarchist thinking and practice has found inspiration in numerous arenas: in widespread outbreaks of popular rebellion against the market discipline imposed upon much of the developing world by the IMF and World Bank; in the pluralistic and democratic political vision emerging out of the Zapatista uprising in Chiapas, Mexico, since 1994; and in the creative and flexible direct action practiced by various European groups. Barbara Epstein—a researcher with a long-standing interest in activist politics—has emphasized that, in North America, anarchists have over the last few decades developed distinctive forms of political action by synthesizing the traditional anarchist concept of close-knit "affinity groups" first developed by Spanish anarchists during the Civil War of the 1930s, tactics of nonviolent civil disobedience from the Gandhian roots of the U.S. civil rights movement, and the Quaker tradition of decision making by group consensus.[31] A combination of these elements has produced the decentralized and leaderless, yet effectively coordinated, forms of protest that spectacularly (if briefly) shut down the Ministerial Conference of the WTO in Seattle in November–December 1999.

Anarchists were highly visible in the Seattle protests largely due to the media attention devoted to the tactic of corporate property destruction adopted by the (relatively few) participants in the militant Black Bloc, a kind of ad hoc anarchist tactical grouping. However, this group was but the most obvious—and arguably the least significant—manifestation of anarchist influence within new movements for global justice (often referred to as the "antiglobalization" movement). In fact, much of the training, preparation, and coordination for the nonviolent direct action that disrupted the WTO meetings in Seattle was carried out by U.S.-based groups such as the Direct Action Network and the Ruckus Society, which were in varying degrees influenced by anarchism. Invoking traditional anarchist values of mutual aid and voluntary cooperation, the Direct Action Network claimed that "A New World Is Possible" and that decentralized but coordinated direct action could help to bring about this "new world." In the years since the Seattle demonstrations, the profound influence of anarchist ideas and practices within the global justice movement have been increasingly widely noted.[32]

An important example of transnational coordination through anarchist-inspired organizational forms is People's Global Action (PGA), which has engaged in militant struggle against neoliberal globalization since the 1998 Geneva mass demonstrations targeting the WTO. Emerging out of intercontinental Zapatista support networks, PGA's founding conference in Geneva in February 1998 was attended by more than 300 representatives of grassroots resistance groups from seventy-one countries around the world. Self-consciously avoiding institutionalized forms of organization based on centralized structures, official leadership, membership rosters, or permanent finances, PGA represents itself as a process rather than a permanent organization—"an evolving coordination" of grassroots groups working together to disrupt global hierarchies and begin to construct a new and better world. The PGA's self-declared "hallmarks" clearly indicate its anarchist heritage. These include rejection of all forms of hierarchy, domination, and discrimination; militant direct action in resistance to oppression; and construction of new forms of social solidarity based on decentralization and autonomy.

In a few short years, PGA has achieved global influence. Its network includes many of the best-known direct action groups around the world, for example, the Direct Action Network and the Montreal Anti-Capitalist Convergence in North America; the KRRS (Karnataka State Farmers' Movement) in India; Ya Basta (Italy) and Reclaim the Streets (UK) in Europe; the Movimento Sem Terra (MST) Landless Workers Movement in Brazil; and a broad and variegated network of associated groups on every populated continent. As a coordinating element linking networks of grassroots resistance, PGA has called for Global Days of Action in support of protests in particular locales aimed at institutions of global capitalist governance. During the September 2000 protests against the IMF/World Bank in Prague, PGA's call for global action prompted demonstrations in 110 cities around the world.

Further reflecting the influence of anarchism, contemporary advocacy for global justice has emphasized not just protest against capitalist globalization, but also the construction of new forms of social organization through which to conduct these struggles. The movement has projected a vision of *prefigurative politics,* in which more democratic forms of social organization are seen as prefigured in, and emerging from, the very forms of organization adopted in the struggles against hierarchy and domination.

David Graeber—an anthropology professor at Yale University and activist closely associated with the anarchist wing of the new global movement—is at pains to disassociate contemporary anarchism from its frightful popular reputation.[33] This reputation has been partly earned by the terrorist tactics adopted during the late nineteenth century, when some anarchists practiced what they called "propaganda of the deed," sensational acts of violence directed against the wealthy and powerful. However, anarchism's public image is also the cumulative result of over 100 years of anti-anarchist caricature and calumny. To counter often-repeated but inaccurate stereotypes that equate anarchy with nihilistic destruction, chaos, and the total absence of organization, Graeber describes anarchism as "a social movement . . . founded above all on opposition to all structures of systematic coercion and a vision of society based on principles of voluntary association, mutual aid and autonomous, self-governing communities":

> In North America especially, this is a movement about reinventing democracy. It is not opposed to organization. It is about creating new forms of organization. It is not lacking in ideology. Those new forms of organization *are* its ideology. It is about creating and enacting horizontal networks instead of top-down structures like states, parties, or corporations; networks based on principles of decentralized, non-hierarchical consensus democracy. Ultimately, it . . . aspires to reinvent daily life as a whole.[34]

Following Bakunin's maxim that "socialism without freedom is tyranny and brutality," anarchist-inspired "libertarian socialists" see freedom and socialism as necessary complements, such that neither is realizable in the absence of the other. Accordingly, many expressions of the new anarchism embrace a dual commitment to *both* grassroots democracy and socialism. For instance, the Anti-Capitalist Convergence of New York envisions a libertarian socialist future in which

> communities and individuals . . . take control over their own lives, and create a new world in which the desire for endless maximization of profit could be replaced by a desire for the full self-realization of human beings: a world in which everyone can have the security of knowing their basic needs will be met, and therefore will be free to contribute to society as they see fit, in sustainable harmony with the earth and the natural world; a

world which would involve pleasures, challenges, and forms of joy and ful-fillment that at present we could hardly imagine.[35]

Anarchism and Marxian socialism—the two major traditions of revolu-tionary politics in the West—continue their long-standing love-hate rela-tionship. Marxist scholar David McNally acknowledges the value of anarchists' stress on grassroots democracy and nonhierarchical modes of organization but criticizes anarchists for their overemphasis on a single set of direct action tactics, their romantic vision of revolution largely discon-nected from the working class and actual struggles within capitalist work-places, and their simplistic equation of reform-oriented demands with cooptation.[36] We conclude that each side has important lessons to learn from the other.

NGOs and Global Reform

One of the politically important developments in the era of globaliza-tion has been the emergence of what is sometimes referred to as global "civil society," including various citizens' groups and NGOs seeking to or-ganize in pursuit of a variety of social and political goals; for example, Greenpeace is a well-known environmental NGO, Amnesty International is active in the area of human rights, and there are many, many others. Whereas at the beginning of the twentieth century there were only 176 international NGOs, by the end of the century their number had risen to nearly 5,500.[37] While not all of these are dedicated to explicitly political goals, NGOs have been important participants in the politics of globaliza-tion. In this section, we discuss some of the reforms proposed by progres-sive think-tanks and NGOs looking for ways to restructure global capitalism so as to arrest the race to the bottom and begin to create a more egalitarian, socially responsible, and democratically accountable global economy.

No Sweat

During the 1990s, activist students, segments of the labor movement, and consumer groups joined together to publicize the relationship between neoliberal globalization and the widespread appearance of sweatshops around the world. In the world of globalizing production, many of the best known brand-name products are not actually manufactured by the corpo-ration whose recognizable brand is prominently displayed on the product. Instead, the big-name firm concentrates on marketing strategies and design of glitzy new products, while actual production is subcontracted to little-known manufacturing firms around the world. The subcontracting system allows great flexibility to the famous-name corporation, which no longer needs to maintain a large and expensive manufacturing workforce through market cycles of boom and bust. And this system focuses intense competitive pressure on the subcontractors, who must meet the strict cost criteria set by the major marketing corporations or lose their contracts to competing producers, each of whom is driven to competitively undercut all the others. Combined with the debt crisis that has beset the developing world for the last two decades and the emphasis on low-wage exports that the IMF has imposed on debtor countries, the restructuring of global production through outsourcing and subcontracting has created a situation in which labor exploitation is severe and endemic. The various forms of exploitation and abuse to which workers may be subjected are collectively referred to as "sweatshop" working conditions.

Antisweatshop activists have sought, with some notable successes, to overcome the structured barrier capitalism imposes between workers and the consumers who buy their products—a market-generated veil of ignorance to which Marx referred as "the fetishism of commodities" (see our discussion in chapter 1). In a global economy in which many major corporations have invested billions in the creation of successful brand names coveted by consumers but do little or no actual manufacturing of products themselves, activists have taken aim at the public image associated with famous brands to exert some leverage over the labor conditions in the factories of their subcontractors. No Sweat activists have sought to inform consumers of the working conditions in factories where famous brand goods are produced and to focus consumer pressure on those brands. Threatening to make a billion-dollar brand name synonymous with degradation and exploitation is a terrifying prospect to major firms whose primary business is the promotion of their brands. A number of major brands including The Gap, Nike, Kathie Lee, Disney, and many others were "outed" as beneficiaries of sweatshop labor. Importantly, activist groups such as the National Labor Committee or Students Against Sweatshops do not pressure corporations simply to drop subcontractors who run sweatshops (which would cost already impoverished workers their jobs) but instead want the big brands to insist that all their suppliers conform to basic standards of minimally acceptable hours, wages, and working conditions. In this way, the No Sweat movement has challenged the depoliticized global economy in which consumers care only about satisfying their own wants and needs, and by upholding basic standards for working people in different parts of the globe have countered some of the downward pressures constituting the global race to the bottom.[38]

Tobin Tax

The globalization of finance has meant that massive volumes of investment capital can move from one place to another on a moment's notice in pursuit of short-term profit. Speculators, who make money by placing massive bets on relatively small fluctuations in international asset values or currency exchange rates, have contributed to global financial instability, as evidenced, for example, in the global financial crises of 1997–1998, which threw millions of people in Asia, Latin America, and Russia into unemployment and dire poverty even as government budgets and social services were slashed. To retard these massive speculative flows and the financial "bubbles," "panics," and destructive economic crises they bring in their wake, organizations such as ATTAC (the French acronym for Association for the Taxation of Financial Transactions for the Aid of Citizens) have campaigned worldwide for a very modest tax (a fraction of 1 percent) on all foreign exchange transactions. Initially conceived by Nobel Prize–winning economist James Tobin (and widely known as the Tobin tax), even a very small percentage tax could be sufficient to erode the fractional profit margins on which speculators depend, while doing little to deter international trade or long-term productive investment (which is not as dependent on very small margins to be profitable). Such a tax has been aptly described as a "speed bump" for transnational finance capital, slowing short-term speculative movements while not blocking necessary transactions. In addition to helping reduce the dangers of global financial speculation, the proceeds from such a tax might be allocated to a global development fund that would support initiatives to help the world's poorest people or to relieve the crushing burden of debt carried by many developing countries.[39]

Visions of Broad-Based Institutional Reform

Author-activists Jeremy Brecher, Tim Costello, and Brendan Smith have argued that the "participants in the movement for globalization from below have varied goals, but the movement's unifying goal is to bring about sufficient democratic control over states, markets, and corporations to permit people and the planet to survive and begin to shape a viable future. . . . Particularly important [as reflections of this emerging possibility] are joint statements that have been drawn up by coalitions whose members have had to take each other's approaches into account."[40] During the 1990s, broad networks of various NGOs and activist groups from across North America came together to formulate a common critique of the North American Free Trade Agreement (NAFTA) and the agenda of neoliberal globalization and to begin to imagine more participatory, egalitarian, democratic, and sustainable alternatives. Between 1993 and 1994, a series of six transnational meetings took place including representatives of labor, environmental, religious, consumer, farm, and women's groups. The product of these meetings was a document entitled *A Just and Sustainable Trade and Development Initiative for the Western Hemisphere*.[41] While initially formulated to address the integration of the Western Hemisphere, the Initiative explicitly extended its horizons to encompass the negotiation of a new global order. To ensure social responsibility and accountability on the part of private firms, it called for detailed codes of conduct to be binding upon international economic actors and reform of the multilateral institutions governing international economic relations so as to safeguard and enforce basic human rights—especially those embodied in the various conventions of the International Labor Organization and the UN Conventions on the Elimination of Racial Discrimination and Discrimination Against Women. New standards such as "the right to a toxic-free workplace and living environment" would be added to this battery of social protections. As a yardstick for the assessment of globalization, the Initiative promoted the criterion of "social sustainability" encompassing not just environmental safeguards but also "the protection of children's welfare, the welfare of families, women's and men's well being, minority and indigenous rights, and the broad geographic sharing of economic gains."[42] As an integral part of this counterhegemonic vision, it prescribed the reduction of inequalities among nations, within nations, and across social categories of gender and race. The culture and self-determination of indigenous groups were to be respected. Provisions for adequate health care, elder and child care, as well as proscriptions of child labor, violence and discrimination against women, and job stereotyping would serve to lessen the economic dependence and double burden experienced by women worldwide. The Initiative called for economic integration to be accompanied by compensatory financing (that is, aid from the richest to the poorest) and debt reduction to lessen economic disparities, forestall the race to the bottom, and raise the floor under all participants in the transnational economy, at the same time enabling more widespread participation in its governance. "Development should be a process in which, to the fullest extent possible, citizens participate and local communities control the initiation and implementation of economic decisions that affect their lives. Achieving this goal will require new mechanisms to make governments, legal institutions, and private corporations more accessible and accountable to the public." Accordingly, the initiative suggested that "new [transnational] institutions should be managed transparently and democratically with broad social, governmental, and private participation."[43] The *Peoples Hemispheric Agreement* of 1998 was drafted by coalitions from Canada, Quebec, Chile, Mexico, and the U.S. and embodies many of the social values and commitments expressed in earlier, trinational documents such as the *Just and Sustainable Trade and Development Initiative*.[44]

In consultation with a number of the activists and NGOs involved in these multinational dialogues, U.S. progressives led by Congressman Bernie Sanders (Ind., VT) in 1999 drafted a document envisioning far-reaching reforms of the global economy.[45] In its opening pages, *The Global Sustainable Development Resolution* declared as its overriding purpose that "the people of the United States and the people and governments of the other nations of the world should take actions to establish democratic control over the global economy."[46] The Resolution declared that unregulated economic globalization has produced the following consequences:

- heightened financial volatility and instability, and an increasing tendency toward financial bubbles, panics, and crises;
- intensified competitive pressures driving a race to the bottom in labor, environmental, and social conditions;
- tendencies toward inadequate aggregate demand (that is, a situation in which consumers do not have enough income to purchase the amount of goods being produced) and underemployment;
- persistent poverty for billions of the world's people;
- massive increases in economic inequality worldwide;
- intensification of discriminatory burdens borne by women, ethnic and racial minorities, and indigenous peoples; and
- last but not least, the undermining of democracy by economic power.

In contrast to this situation, the Resolution envisioned a global economy that would be framed by such principles as "democracy at every level of government from the local to the global," human rights (including "labor, social, environmental, economic and cultural rights") for all people, environmental sustainability, and "economic advancement for the most oppressed and exploited parts of the population, including women, immigrants, racial and ethnic minorities and indigenous peoples."[47] Sanders and his collaborators propose reforming international economic institutions so that voting rights are based on population rather than wealth (so as to give the poorest a greater voice), increasing the openness of their decision-making procedures, and explicitly including in their deliberations "labor unions, environmental groups, women's organizations, development organizations, and other major sectors of civil society in each affected country."[48] Further, the drafters call for the creation of Commissions on the Global Economy at national and transnational levels to encourage broad public dialogue (explicitly including the various elements of civil society) on globalization and alternative possible futures. The drafters further envision measures to re-regulate capital and tax foreign exchange transactions in order to reduce short-term speculative capital flows and encourage long-term investment in socially accountable and sustainable development. They call for the cancellation of debts owed by the poorest countries and the reorientation of international financial institutions toward domestic economic growth and full employment rather than domestic austerity and export-led growth. And they propose enforceable codes of conduct designed to "establish public control and citizen sovereignty over global corporations."[49] Labor, environmental, and social standards would be inscribed in these codes of conduct, as well as in the governing principles of international financial institutions and trade agreements. According to Sanders's office, the Resolution was endorsed by at least seventy NGOs, including many that have been active in resistance to neoliberal globalization, such as Public Citizen's Global Trade Watch, Campaign for Labor Rights, Fifty Years Is Enough, Global Exchange, Interhemispheric Resource Center, International Labor Rights Fund, Institute for Policy Studies, United Electrical Workers, Friends of the Earth, and the Center for International Environmental Law.

Canadian author-activists Maude Barlow and Tony Clarke have advanced similar sorts of reform proposals based on "Citizens' Inquiries"—a series of public discussions organized by the Council of Canadians. According to Barlow and Clarke, localization is a core principle of this agenda: "Democratic rights and the common good can be protected best through the creation of local sustainable communities, in which local resources are used by local people to produce goods and services for distribution close to home, within ecological limits."[50] Coexisting somewhat uneasily with this emphasis on economic localization is their call for "living and acting in a spirit of international solidarity" in order to construct a more democratic and enabling global order—one that would combine representative and participatory forms of democracy at varying scales to "maximize citizen participation in public policy making" from the local to the national and transnational levels.[51] More specifically, they propose creating a global environment more conducive to local reforms. They call for reconstructing the global trade regime to safeguard public services (especially health, education, water, and energy), restrict the ability of corporations to commodify social knowledge via "intellectual property rights," encourage sustainable agriculture and prevent the dumping of agricultural surpluses by the rich countries into the markets of the poor (a practice that drives poor and less "efficient" farmers from their land), and allow for increased national regulation of foreign investment. Further, they call for the re-regulation of global finance and the creation of "speed bump measures" to retard the speculative capital flows that have generated repeated financial crises around the world. And they propose the rechartering of transnational corporations to make their continuing existence contingent upon social responsibility and accountability. Corporations with track records of environmental, labor, and/or human rights abuses would risk losing their legal right to exist. "Weaving its way through all of these demands is the call for a fundamental redistribution of wealth and power. Developing a new democracy along these lines at local, national, and international levels is the only possible antidote to corporate globalization."[52] While they share with the anarchists an understanding of social change as emerging from transnational social movement activism and the development of new forms of social power, Barlow and Clarke explicitly contrast their own prescriptions for multilevel democratization with the strongly decentralized visions of the anarchist-oriented wings of the global justice movement.

Toward Global Parliamentary Governance?

George Monbiot, an author-activist who has been deeply involved in the global justice movement, has recently staked out a position openly critical of both the anarchist-inspired and localizing tendencies within the movement. To those who would replace the global economy with relatively self-sufficient, protected local markets, Monbiot objects that this would not reduce the asymmetry of power that underlies global economic inequalities: "If all nations were to protect their economies, the wealth of the rich ones might be diminished but the poverty of the poor ones would not. We would, if we follow this prescription, lock the poor world into destitution."[53] Monbiot is then led to contemplate directly a political reconstruction of the world order centered on the creation of more egalitarian global institutions:

> The four principal projects are these: a democratically elected world parliament; a democratized United Nations General Assembly, which captures the powers now vested in the Security Council; an International Clearing Union [harkening back to the world monetary system envisioned by J. M.

Keynes at the close of World War II], which automatically discharges trade deficits and prevents the accumulation of debt; a Fair Trade organization, which restrains the rich while emancipating the poor.[54]

Such proposals for global government would, of course, outrage the various anarchist-inspired segments of the global justice movement, all of whom share in common a profound distrust of institutionalized, concentrated, and hierarchical forms of power. Yet Monbiot steadfastly claims that such power, wielded for egalitarian purposes, offers the only hope for reversing the massive inequalities that characterize the modern world. "The reason that democratic governance is more likely to deliver justice than anarchism is that it possesses the capacity for coercion: the rich and powerful can be restrained, by the coercive measures of the state, from oppressing the rest of us."[55] Monbiot's vision of redistributive global government has been subjected to scorching criticism from Grahame Thompson, who argues that it is premised upon a naively utopian view of world politics that overlooks the continuing significance and power of nation-states:

> Neither the US nor other rich countries would passively consent to radical change on the Monbiot model. Their citizens—not just their political and corporate leaders—will demand protection and security against such an eventuality. They are likely to feel better represented from within their states than by any World Representative Parliament or reformed UN General Assembly.[56]

As Thompson sees it, Monbiot has simply imagined an idealized vision of an alternative world (which may or may not strike others as ideal) without paying sufficient attention to the critical issue of how we get there from here, that is, the currently existing political actors and processes that might plausibly bring such a world into being. In light of contemporary political realities, Thompson suggests, "we are left with one feasible alternative option; that it will be national governments that take the lead in any further extensions of international governance, on an ad hoc and limited functional basis rather than in terms of some comprehensive global initiative."[57] In Thompson's view, this would entail a plurality of more specialized institutions at various scales, with international cooperation at the regional level playing a leading role in their construction and maintenance.

Anarchist-oriented activists have been bitterly critical of the NGOs. Playing off the popular chant of grassroots street protesters—"This is what democracy looks like!"—some anarchist-oriented critics have blasted the reformist orientation and hierarchical, bureaucratized politics, which they see as characteristic of the NGO sector, taunting them with a parodied version of the chant: "This is what bureaucracy looks like."[58] Others, however, have suggested that the apparent dilemma of *reform or revolution* may well be a false dichotomy. American radical Michael Albert has argued that those anarchists who equate any institutions whatever with domination are mistaken: "The mistake is that while institutional roles that compel people to deny their humanity or the humanity of others are, of course, abominable, institutions that permit people to express their humanity more fully and freely are not abominable at all, but part and parcel of a just social order." Accordingly, he advocates what he calls "non-reformist reforms":

> What's needed . . . isn't to have no reforms, which would simply capitulate the playing field to elites, but to fight for reforms that are non-reformist, that is, to fight for reforms that we [social movements] conceive, seek, and implement in ways leading activists to seek still more gains in a trajectory of change leading ultimately to new institutions.[59]

Here—in the important distinction between top-down reforms, which reproduce hierarchies of domination, and bottom-up reforms, which may further empower those seeking to overturn relations that subordinate and exploit them—we begin to glimpse the potential common ground among anarchists, Marxian socialists, and NGO reformers opposing neoliberal globalization. Marxist scholar-activist Alex Callinicos calls for "transitional reforms"—"reforms that emerge from the realities of existing struggles but whose implementation in the current context would challenge capitalist economic relations."[60] He advocates a number of measures put forth by NGOs: regulation of global finance; Tobin tax on foreign exchange transactions; debt forgiveness for poor countries; preservation and expansion of public services around the world; environmental protection measures; defense of civil liberties; and demilitarization. To this list, however, he adds measures to lessen the coercive power of capital over working people: a "universal basic income" to reduce the wage dependence of workers and thus enhance their bargaining power with employers, and a reduction of the work week in order to free workers to participate in democratic deliberations and political activity. Taken together, Callinicos suggests, such "transitional reforms" will decommodify important parts of our lives, begin to undermine capitalism's drive for competitive accumulation, and prepare the ground for a transformation of capitalist social relations into something quite different, more egalitarian and democratic. The illuminating writings of Albert and Callinicos strongly suggest that if we conceive of social change as a process, there need be no hard and fast separation between visions of fundamental social transformation embraced by revolutionaries and pragmatic strategies of institutional change put forth by reformers. In this view, there exists some potential common ground among the anarchist, socialist, and NGO wings of the movement.

Another World in the Making? The World Social Forum

The tensions and possibilities inherent in the global justice movement have been clearly evident in its major regular convocation, the World Social Forum (WSF). Conceived as a grassroots-oriented and democratic alternative coinciding with the annual meetings of the elite WEF in Davos, the WSF has grown from around ten thousand attendees in its 2001 inaugural meeting to about 100,000 participants in 2003 (Porto Alegre, Brazil) and 2004 (Mumbai, India). Reflecting the influence of anarchist thought within the global justice movement, the WSF does not represent itself as a unified political organization seeking to advance a single program; rather it claims to be "a plural, diversified, non-confessional, non-governmental and non-party context" for transnational dialogue about alternative possible globalizations.[61] As two participant-observer scholars express it, the WSF "is not an agent, but is instead a pedagogical and political space that enables learning, networking and political organizing" among those who share a basic belief that another world is possible.[62]

Although some have suggested that people of color, women, and the global poor are underrepresented at WSF meetings, we may recognize that there is room for improvement on this score and still appreciate the diversity of issues and perspectives represented in WSF deliberations.[63] Discussions involve the global economy, environment and water, health and medicine, food and agriculture, urbanization, indigenous peoples, cultural diversity and the media, discrimination, violence against women, militarization and war, democracy, and more. The WSF Charter of Principles summarizes the underlying premise of these wide-ranging discussions as follows: "The global movement for justice faces enormous challenges: its fight for peace and collective security implies confronting poverty, discrimination and domination and working for the creation of an alternative sustainable society."[64]

William Fisher and Thomas Ponniah have identified a series of tensions, evident in WSF deliberations, that coexist with these powerful underlying commonalties:

- Some participants call for reforming global institutions, whereas others understand their mission as the revolutionary abolition of such institutions (although it is significant, we have indicated above that we do not see this division as insurmountable in principle).
- What is the appropriate scale of political action and institutional change: local, national, global, or all of these?
- Environmentalists push for a reduction of the resource consumption

and pollution generated by economic growth, whereas others (especially unions) are deeply concerned with preserving jobs and maintaining incomes.

* Labor movements from the rich countries of the global North have called for human rights and labor standards to be incorporated into global institutions, while representatives from the global South suspect that Northern workers are less interested in global human rights and more interested in preserving their own jobs.
* Are advocates of allegedly universal values actually seeking global recognition for the values espoused by globally dominant wealthy societies? Is it possible to construct a global normative order which embraces and preserves a variety of value systems, including those of the world's marginalized peoples?[65]

Instead of suggesting that either unity or division will prevail in the WSF, Fisher and Ponniah harken back to Marcos's poetic vision of a world containing many worlds. They suggest that it is the continuous balancing of commonality and difference through democratic dialogue that represents the real heart of the WSF process: "A contemporary counter-hegemony has to embrace a respect for difference without precluding a capacity to articulate a common vision. . . . In our reading, the convergence of difference among the anticorporate globalization movements lies less in a shared vision of an outcome than in a shared commitment to a process . . . *the reinvention of democracy.*"[66]

Conclusion

Globalization entails changes in the political and cultural, as well as economic, aspects of social life. This chapter sketches some of the dialectics of power emerging out of contemporary globalization. A Gramscian-inflected HM enables an understanding of globalizing capitalism, its relations of power and structures of governance, as the product of struggles—at once material and ideological—among concretely situated social agents. We saw that globally dominant social groups—to whom Gramsci might have referred as a "historic bloc" pursuing a transnational hegemonic project—use the WEF and similar venues to imagine a global order supremely hospitable to corporate capital and to develop strategies by means of which to achieve such a world. Representing transnational corporate capital and their political allies, the WEF played an important part in the formulation of an ideology of "entrepreneurship in the public interest" which seeks to rationalize global corporate power and to legitimate it through a discourse of "globalization with a human face."

As the emergent neoliberal historical bloc has sought to (re)produce its social powers on an increasingly global scale, they have encountered recurrent bouts of more or less explicitly political resistance from a variety of social agents (some explicitly class-identified but many others not) who have challenged neoliberal representations and called into question not just the agenda of the neoliberal globalization, but also the legitimacy of the implicitly capitalist social powers underlying it. The ideological cement that bound the movement together and enabled it to begin to envision alternative possible worlds was a culture of solidarity, mutual respect, and reciprocity that transcended national boundaries and formal citizenship. The global justice movement began, in short, to (re)construct a transnational common sense and corresponding forms of political organization and activity. The future meanings of the global justice movement will be determined in large part by struggles over popular common sense in various locales around the world, and whether activists and "organic intellectuals" embedded within those sites are able to articulate globalization/solidarity in opposition to strong currents of globalization/competitiveness or globalization/nationalism.

GENDER, CLASS, AND THE
TRANSNATIONAL POLITICS
OF SOLIDARITY

> Why was Angelo de la Cruz saved? Because I stuck to my oath.
> Since I first became President in 2001, my declared foreign pol-
> icy focus has been to protect the vital interests of the nation,
> including our eight million overseas Filipinos.
>
> —Gloria Macapagal-Arroyo, State of the Nation Address,
> July 26, 2004

Angelo de la Cruz and Overseas Filipino Workers

In mid-July 2004 Angelo de la Cruz, a forty-six-year-old Filipino truck
driver and employee of a Saudi firm working in Iraq, was kidnapped by a
group identifying itself as the Khaled Bin Al-Walid Squadrons of the Islamic Army of Iraq. In what had become a familiar news event, a foreigner
had been kidnapped by militants who demanded withdrawal of troops or
other changes in government policy of the victim's country. What was un-
familiar was the reaction of the government in question. Almost all governments similarly threatened (U.S., U.K., Italy, etc.) had refused to even
consider such demands and condemned any country that would "negotiate
with terrorists." President Gloria Macapagal-Arroyo, in a decision harshly
criticized by most governments in the Iraqi occupation coalition, essentially agreed to the demands of the kidnappers in order to save the life of
Angelo de la Cruz.

Why did Macapagal-Arroyo agree to "speed up" the withdrawal of Philippine forces in Iraq? Was this simply the case of a weak government giving in to the demands of terrorists? Though often presented as such in

establishment media circles, the truth is more complex. Although the government of the Philippines maintained the decision was only the change of a time schedule for removal of forces, there is no denying that the government changed its policy under the threat of the execution of one of its citizens. At first glance such a decision seems shortsighted for a government that has waged an internal battle with Islamic separatists for decades.

Macapagal-Arroyo changed government policy because the death of de la Cruz would have resulted in massive public outrage at the government's inability to protect an Overseas Filipino Worker (OFW). Had de la Cruz been killed by his captors, it is possible Macapagal-Arroyo would have been forced from power. The reasons for this public interest in a single OFW are complex but stem from the fact that de la Cruz was a symbol of the nearly 10 percent of Filipino citizens who are living and working abroad. This individual OFW was like millions of other Filipinos, women and men, working abroad—poor, desperate to provide income for the family, and hopeful of a better future for themselves and their families by earning money abroad, even under very dangerous conditions. Further, the government of the Philippines is dependent on OFWs in ways that make the protection of their minimal safety imperative for even a modicum of legitimacy. We discuss the Philippines as an example of a new form of globalized state below. Angelo de la Cruz's experience demonstrates how one aspect of contemporary globalization—migration—is always present in the background of international events, even "the war on terror."

Migration

As the previous chapter demonstrates, there is much more to globalization than goods and services moving across borders. In the rush to analyze the movement of commodities and finance, scholars often focus their attention on the disadvantage that "fixed" labor faces in a world of mobile, quicksilver capital. Yet an analysis of contemporary globalization would be deficient without a discussion of migration. The globalization debate has been surprisingly devoid of a sustained analysis of migration patterns as evidence of contemporary globalization. Indeed, for globalization skeptics absolute magnitudes of migration are cited as evidence for the greater integration of the "first wave" during the late nineteenth and early twentieth centuries. For example, Hirst and Thompson claim "(t)he era of mass family migration has yet to repeat itself in the way it operated in the period up to the First World War" and also discount the smaller levels of contemporary migration as made up of many migrant laborers and refugees.[1] To be sure, the levels of migration from Europe to the United States were greater in absolute and relative (as percent of receiving population) terms during the first wave. Castles and Miller claim that from 1861 to 1920 some 30 million immigrants made their way to the U.S., more than the total of immigrants from 1920 to the present.[2] Yet it is precisely the different *form* and *process* of migration manifested by contemporary globalization that makes it crucial to understanding that globalization. For example, the explosion of contract and undocumented migration is directly attributable to processes of globalization not existent in the first wave. As discussed more fully below, temporary migration, far from being inconsequential because of the eventual return of the migrant, is transforming the boundaries of sending states, altering the calculus of state policy makers, and serving as a vital source of the external finance necessary for servicing debt and importing oil. Those who would seek to downplay the significance of migrant labor (who will presumably return to their home country at some point) miss one of the crucial elements of why contemporary globalization is different from previous forms.

Another aspect of contemporary migration patterns that serves to differentiate it from previous waves is the increasing *feminization* of migration. By feminization of migration we mean both the increasing number of female migrants since the 1960s and the sectoral nature of much temporary migration—particularly the putatively feminine sectors such as domestic work, nursing, and other "caregiving" labor. Though reliable statistical data prior to 1960 are lacking, recent studies suggest that since 1960 the number of female migrants has grown to roughly 50 percent of all migrants.[3] Rising numbers of female migrants, particularly temporary (contract) migrants, are reflective of the historically specific nature of contemporary migration.

Migration has become a controversial subject in many developed countries as increasing immigration is seen as a threat to wages, employment, and job security among workers already residing in those countries. Even though numerous studies indicate that immigration often has a trivial or even positive effect on wages, immigration remains a hot-button political issue.[4] Among the reasons immigration has provoked so much debate is the large number of immigrants from less developed countries (LDCs) to wealthier countries, many of whom are fleeing economic crisis arguably created or exacerbated by neoliberal restructuring (see our discussion of this in chapter 2). Obviously, when culture and ethnicity are mixed with difficult economic times, there is the potential for creating scapegoats. Complex structural forces are easily ignored when bad times can be blamed on "bad people," aliens who are said to be "taking our jobs" and "distorting our culture." Scapegoating of alien others is a staple of the kinds of economic, cultural, and racial nationalisms that have reasserted themselves throughout the developed world in response to globalization.[5]

Such simplistic and reductionist accounts are not absent from the academy. Indeed, the eminent political scientist Samuel P. Huntington of Harvard University has recently advanced the notion that "America was created by 17th and 18th century settlers who were overwhelmingly white, British, and Protestant. Their values, institutions, and culture provided the foundation for and shaped the development of the United States in the following centuries." Huntington goes on to argue that Hispanic immigration to the U.S., particularly Mexican immigration, "threatens to divide the United States into two peoples, two cultures, and two languages." Why is this a threat? Because, according to Huntington, American culture and identity are essentially English in language and political culture (for example, English concepts of the rule of law, individualism, and the so-called Protestant work ethic). Further insights about this alleged threat are provided by the observation that "the single most immediate and serious challenge to Americans' traditional identity comes from the immense and continuing immigration from Latin America, especially from Mexico, and the fertility rates of these immigrants compared to black and white American natives."[6] It seems Huntington's thesis is motivated by a fear of Spanish-speaking Catholic immigrants who reject the Protestant work ethic and have too many babies. Based as it is upon crude cultural stereotypes, Huntington's latest work on immigration and American identity would be easily dismissed as a laughably simplistic depiction of a complex issue were it not so dangerous.

Huntington's work could be criticized by noting that non-Anglo-Protestants indeed had a large role in "creating America," whether in actually performing the labor that built the country or making demands that the American creed of equality before the law that Huntington speaks of should become something more than an abstract declaration of principles. As discussed in chapter 1, capitalist societies are marked by the juridical promise of freedom and equality before the law, but the realization of that promise is often problematic, requiring long struggle against entrenched social power and prevailing attitudes. For now, let us propose that an understanding of contemporary immigration requires a structural, more holistic analysis to be understood in all its complexity.

Let us think about the question of what a structural account of migration would look like. As opposed to a reductionist account, which focuses on individuals and the decisions they make about migration, a structural account analyzes broader forces that can have an effect on migration. For example, a structural account of the number of Mexican immigrants (regardless of status as documented/undocumented) who enter the U.S. in search of employment would also consider things like segmented labor markets and the demand for cheap labor in the United States, the economic conditions in Mexico, and government policies in both countries that affect these and other variables. For instance, no understanding of Mexican migration would be complete without including a discussion of Mexico's dramatic neoliberal restructuring in the 1980s. This shift in government policy sought to privatize many state institutions, reduce government spending, create export-led growth, and generate economic dynamism by integrating Mexico more fully into global financial and production circuits. In keeping with the underlying goals of the neoliberal agenda, the creation of a more "flexible" labor force was integral to restructuring in Mexico. To the extent that it succeeded in reducing stability in the labor market, neoliberal restructuring is at least partially responsible for the insecurity that makes emigration more attractive to working people struggling to make ends meet.

This is only one example of how a structural account may broaden analysis of migration. Importantly, a more structural account allows us to appreciate the manner in which LDCs increasingly *create* migrants to generate external finance. The Philippines may be the most dramatic example of this trend, but LDCs are increasingly recognizing the benefit of creating migrant flows to wealthier countries to generate remittance income—the foreign currency earned by overseas workers and sent back home to their families and thus remitted to their home countries in the form of "hard currency" that can be used to pay international debts or acquire imports. For many countries remittance income is now the primary source of external finance, and the World Bank's *Global Development Finance Report 2004* indicates:

> Remittance flows are the second-largest source, behind FDI [Foreign Direct Investment], of external funding for developing countries. In 2001, workers' remittances receipts of developing countries stood at $72.3 billion, much higher than total official flows and private non-FDI flows, and 42 percent of total FDI flows to developing countries.[7]

What is not immediately apparent from the above is the manner in which some forms of migration, particularly temporary contract migration, have been created by states with the explicit intent of creating remittance flows and generating hard currency. LDCs have been driven to find new ways to earn additional hard currency by the pressures that globalization has exerted upon them, such as the OPEC-engineered oil price increases of the

1970s or the financial shock of soaring global interest rates on burdensome sovereign debt in the early 1980s (for discussion of the "debt crisis," see chapter 2). Whatever the motivation, LDCs are increasingly viewing their population itself as a potential "export." Of course, this is entirely consistent with neoliberal visions of globalization that call for reduced transaction costs and less friction as goods and services move across national borders—only now we are talking about human labor as one more commodity involved in the circuits of global accumulation.

The World Bank's perspective on this phenomenon is not merely descriptive but also *prescriptive* in calling for more of this particular export. After noting that reducing transaction costs on remittance transfers and other technical improvements could increase the flow of funds to LDCs, the Bank notes:

> Facilitating international mobility is an even more crucial—and controversial—means of increasing remittance flows to developing countries. Greater international migration could generate substantial benefits to the world economy.[8]

The substantial benefits the Bank speaks of relate to the cheaper labor immigrant workers supply to developed economies, the increased flows of external finance that emigrants will presumably send home, and the higher wages that the emigrants are able to obtain by working in countries where wage levels are generally higher than at home. Clearly, the World Bank's understanding of this process is driven by the same market logic that underpins much of the neoliberal version of economic globalization. That is, liberalization policies that reduce the friction of goods, services, and finance as they move across borders will inexorably lead to greater welfare for the countries making the exchange and hence, greater global welfare. The World Bank's conception of increasing global welfare driven by remittances of workers abroad is the logical extension of the free trade conception of neoclassical economics. As represented by renowned international economist Jagdish Bhagwati, the free trade position "rests on the extension to an open economy of the case for market-determined allocation of resources. If market prices reflect 'true' or social costs, then clearly Adam Smith's invisible hand can be trusted to guide us to efficiency; and free trade can correspondingly be shown to be the optimal way to choose trade (and associated domestic production)."[9] The market logic is clear enough here. However, with regard to the process of generating remittances, the hand that guides the process is not an invisible one—it is the quite effective hand of the state, and the products being traded are people. According to this logic, when migrant workers move from LDCs to developed economies for temporary work contracts, it is merely a sort of "arbitrage"—that is, moving commodities from places where they are plentiful and cheap to places where they are more scarce and in demand. In 2003 President Bush spoke of creating a guest worker program in the United States. Clearly, this form of migration is different from previous waves oriented toward permanent settlement and is reflective of contemporary globalization, neo-liberal restructuring, and the drive for more "flexible" labor arrangements.

The Philippines

An observant passenger arriving at Ninoy Aquino International Airport in Manila will quickly notice a few surprising things. First, there are a number of lines at passport control, customs, and security marked "Overseas Filipino Worker Express Line." Another surprise is the number of unexpected air carriers on the tarmac: a quick glance reveals Saudi Arabian Airlines, Qatar Airways, Kuwait Airways, and a number of other Persian Gulf airlines. A visitor may wonder why so many Middle Eastern tourists would want to come to the Philippines, as lovely as it is. Of course, these carriers are mostly filled with OFWs going to or returning from jobs in the Middle East. For example, there are estimated to be nearly one million Filipino contract workers in Saudi Arabia alone.[10]

The Philippines represent a paradigmatic example of the state-driven policy of generating remittance finance through a determined state policy. While small-scale migration of various sorts has been seen in the Philippines for many decades, the large-scale migration of temporary workers overseas began only in 1974 in response to the oil shock of 1973.[11] Like many LDCs who are importers of oil, the Philippines was particularly vulnerable to the quadrupling of oil prices following the OPEC-induced oil shock. The government of President Ferdinand Marcos established an innovative approach to dealing with the balance-of-payments crisis that quickly followed. In what was originally envisioned as a temporary program to generate hard-currency remittance income, the Philippine government established a policy of encouraging Filipinos to work overseas for fixed periods of time (established by contract before leaving the Philippines). Ironically, or perhaps fittingly, the first region to receive large numbers of Filipino workers was the Middle East, especially oil-exporting countries suddenly flush with enormous revenues and possessing populations not inclined to perform manual labor. Essentially, the Philippines dealt with the massive increase in price for oil imports by trading workers for oil.

What was envisioned as a temporary policy became permanent and an essential part of Philippine economic policy.[12] State institutions like the Overseas Worker Welfare Administration (OWWA) and the Philippine Overseas Employment Administration (POEA) were developed to promote and service a Filipino workforce overseas. To further encourage the outflow of contract workers the government has consistently deployed a discourse describing overseas workers as "heroes of the nation." Through media campaigns, government policy pronouncements, and a steady repetition within government offices, all Filipinos are encouraged to take pride in these "heroes." Surprisingly, the motivation of the government is not always concealed. For example, the Philippine Overseas Employment Administration website announces the annual Bagong Bayani (literally, "our new heroes") award in a manner that should make it clear to even the casual observer what the government's stake in this process is:

> The Bagong Bayani Awards (BBA) is an annual search for the country's outstanding Overseas Filipino Workers (OFWs), as new heroes of our time. We pay tribute to their significant efforts in fostering goodwill among peoples of the world, enhancing the image of the Filipino as a competent and responsible worker and contributing to the nation's foreign exchange earnings.[13]

To appreciate the truly global phenomenon that Filipino migrant labor has become, we can look at the distribution and estimated totals in table 4.1, provided by the Philippine government.

The numbers here are striking. Out of a total population of 84 million, approximately 7.8 million are working abroad—roughly one in ten Filipinos. The other striking figure is the $7.6 billion of remittance income generated by these workers, or roughly 10 percent of the Gross Domestic Product (GDP) of the Philippines. The regional breakdown demonstrates that temporary contract workers are the norm in most regions of the world, with only the Americas (overwhelmingly U.S./Canada) showing large numbers of permanent migrants.

To bring home the point of the Philippines as an example of a state that actively seeks to create the export of labor, we can briefly examine the POEA, a government bureau charged with managing the documentation of overseas workers, encouraging overseas temporary migration, creating export markets, marketing Filipino workers abroad, and generally managing the outflow of temporary migrants. The POEA, operating on a slim annual budget of approximately $3.5 million, processes millions of overseas workers while actively seeking new markets for OFWs in a variety of sectors. While such occupations as domestic workers, construction labor, and

Table 4.1   Estimate of Overseas Filipino Workers (December 2003)

Region	Permanent	Temporary	Irregular	TOTAL
Africa	318	53,706	16,955	70,979
S. and E. Asia	85,570	944,129	503,173	1,532,872
Middle East	2,290	1,361,409	108,150	1,471,849
Europe	165,030	459,042	143,810	767,882
Americas	2,386,036	286,103	709,676	3,381,815
Oceania	226,168	55,814	31,001	312,983
Sea-based		216,031		216,031
Region Unspecified		8,767		8,767
World Total	2,865,412	3,385,001	1,512,765	7,763,178

Population of Philippines (2003): 84.6 million

Value of Remittances (2003): $7.6 Billion

GDP of the Philippines (2003): $80.6 Billion

Source: Commission on Filipinos Overseas, Philippine Department of Foreign Affairs, and Central Bank of the Philippines, at www.poea.gov.ph/docs/ofwStock2003.doc.

seafarers (labor for shipping) are no surprise, the POEA also actively seeks markets for teachers, information technology specialists, highly skilled health care workers, and other skilled positions.

The POEA and the other government agencies dedicated to the promotion and welfare of OFWs combine to make the Philippines the paradigmatic example of a managed labor-export system. While no other country comes close to the same level of government involvement, many other countries in the region view the Philippine contract migration model as something to emulate. The International Labor Organization (ILO) and the International Organization for Migration (IOM) have helped organize visits to the POEA by a number of countries in the region (e.g., Thailand, Indonesia, Sri Lanka, Vietnam) as well as countries not usually thought of as major labor exporting countries, such as Jordan and Azerbaijan. Although it could be argued that such training and information exchange can lead to competition from other countries (thereby putting downward pressure on wages), POEA officials are hopeful that coordination with other labor-exporting countries will lead to cooperation in upward pressure on wages and working conditions. The dramatic increase of temporary migrants from Indonesia has resulted in large numbers of Indonesians competing with Filipinos in various markets. In response to this competition the POEA "forged a formal alliance with Indonesia on January 18, 2003, the first bilateral agreement with a labor sending country, for the promotion and protection of the welfare and rights of Filipino and Indonesian migrant workers."[14] Regardless of the strategy, it is clear that more, not less, contract labor migration will be on offer in the foreseeable future.

Migrant Domestic Workers

There is significant diversity in the kinds of work performed by Filipinos who migrate for temporary contract work. Though the majority work in "unskilled" professions, there are also medical personnel and technically trained migrants. A crucial sector that comprises the majority of women migrants from the Philippines (and other Southeast Asian states) is that of domestic worker (also referred to as domestic helpers or "maids"). Throughout the Middle East and the Asia-Pacific, millions of migrant women labor as domestic workers. Filipina domestic workers served as the vanguard in this form of migrant labor as part of the general export of labor from the Philippines discussed above. Indonesian domestic workers became more prominent in the mid- to late 1980s as the Indonesian government began to embrace the logic of remittance income as a reliable source of external finance. Other domestic worker exporting states include Thailand, Sri Lanka, Bangladesh, and India.

Christine Chin's *In Service and Servitude* (1998) examines the manner in which the state project of Malaysian development and modernity was, and is, based at least in part on the use of Filipina and Indonesian domestic workers. Rhacel Salazar Parreñas's *Servants of Globalization* (2001) investigates Filipina domestic workers in Italy and the U.S. and demonstrates that while geography may produce particular challenges, the essential difficulties faced by foreign domestic workers are universal. Nicole Constable's groundbreaking work *Maid to Order in Hong Kong* (1997) examines the phenomenon of Filipina domestic workers in Hong Kong through in-depth interviews. This and other ethnographic work demonstrates that while Filipina domestic workers are at a severe disadvantage in terms of the power differential they face, they are often capable of creative acts of resistance at both the micro level of the conditions of work in the household and the macro level of contesting state policies on wages, conditions of employment, and contracts. The most detailed attempt at linking this phenomenon to globalization proper is the work of Chang and Ling in "Globalization and Its Intimate Other: Filipina Domestic Workers in Hong Kong." They contrast "techno-muscular capitalism (TMC)," the more traditional understanding of globalization as based on globalized production, finance, and trade, with "the regime of labor intimacy," which represents the world of domestic work and is "the intimate other" of TMC. Of course, the "techno-muscular capitalism," which is the more visible side of globalization, is dependent on its "intimate other" for survival in that the conditions of production and trade require the continual reproduction of the household, labor, and the family.[15]

This scholarship has contributed to a better understanding of the phenomenon of migrant domestic workers, *especially* with regard to how deeply gendered this process is. Some of the findings are not surprising. This form of work leads to a particular kind of isolation in which the overwhelming majority of a domestic worker's time is spent within the intimate space of an(other)'s home. The intimate nature of the work combined with the disregard or negligence of authorities leaves these women particularly vulnerable to physical and sexual abuse. Spending many years away from home with only occasional short visits results in estrangement from friends, family, children, or spouses—often the very people for whom the worker is making the sacrifice of working abroad. Of course, the low regard for this form of work and lack of protection in the receiving state also result in the frequent denial of wages, disregard of contractual obligations of the employer, and other forms of labor abuse.

What is even more compelling about this work are the unexpected findings that are driven by the feminist nature of much of this scholarship. Let us mention just two of these. First, this form of labor takes significant pressure off the receiving state to provide child care, particularly when societies are undergoing a transformation in which middle-class women are entering the workforce in large numbers and can employ immigrant women as child care providers.[16] Particularly in the Asia-Pacific region, where dynamic growth in the 1970s–1980s led to more opportunity for women to enter into waged labor, the possibility of hiring a domestic worker allows opportunities that might otherwise be difficult for the household to manage.

A second significant finding relates to the inversion of the private–public border as traditionally understood with regard to labor. Most workers are in public space while working and private (intimate) space while home. For domestic workers the situation is inverted: They work in the intimate, private space of another's household and, since their own homes are far away, what little leisure time they have is spent in public space (away from the private household in which they work). In areas where population density and numbers of domestic workers are high (such as Hong Kong or Singapore), this can result in public space being redefined on particular days when domestic workers are off work and can congregate together in large numbers (usually Sundays). In Hong Kong this has resulted in heightening tensions around domestic worker programs as native

Hong Kong citizens sometimes react in racist and nativist ways (particularly during periods of economic crisis).[17] Scholars of the transition from feudalism to capitalism have noted how the factory system sowed the seeds for labor organization by bringing workers together for extended periods of time. In a similar fashion, domestic workers are doing the same when they are away from work. Since they have only limited public space in which to spend their free time, they tend to congregate there in large numbers. These gatherings provide the very real perception of the possibility of collective empowerment, allow for the networking and organizing that unions and advocacy groups rely on, and serve as a space for collective discussions of the conditions of employment.

Intersectional Politics

Any discussion of migrant domestic workers must face a number of analytical hurdles. Gender, class, race, and nation are all part of the story and, we argue, cannot be understood in isolation. We adopt the notion of "intersectional politics" as one way to theorize the processes that surround migrant domestic work. Scholars of these issues have a tendency to focus on a particular variable—such as gender or class—often to the exclusion of the others. We argue that to do so illuminates aspects of these processes but at significant costs. Given limitations of space and our own intellectual shortcomings we no doubt make similar omissions in this discussion. However, we remain committed to an understanding of globalization deeply influenced, but not wholly determined, by HM. In chapter 1 we noted that HM, especially early variants, has often ignored or consciously excluded gender or race as categories that are secondary to class. We acknowledged this shortcoming of HM and argued that the theoretical leverage provided by HM is enhanced, not diminished, by a more open-ended approach. In the same fashion that feminist scholars rightly claim that ignoring gender impoverishes social theory, we claim that ignoring class, the division of labor, and the social organization of production renders social theory incomplete.

Domestic work is an "intimate" activity in that it takes place in the home. Feminist scholars have consistently, and correctly, argued that patriarchal social relations have obscured the necessary labor that is required to reproduce the household. Cooking, cleaning, and other forms of intimate labor have disproportionately fallen to women and have been systematically undervalued. The sexual division of labor within capitalist societies has resulted in women performing a "double shift" where they are expected to perform labor necessary to maintain the household while often also earning a wage outside the household. In those societies where capitalist social relations have resulted in industrialization and sustained levels of economic growth, the "dull compulsion of the economic" has created conditions where the double shift is a necessity for many women.

However, all households are not the same. One of the defining characteristics of capitalism is a form of class differentiation wherein some households have the means to *purchase* the labor necessary to maintain the household. Particularly in households where children are present and household income is high enough to do so, domestic work can be transformed into a waged relationship by hiring someone from outside the household. As mentioned above, when the economies of Hong Kong, Singapore, and Taiwan experienced rates of growth that drew more women into the workforce, domestic labor was often taken care of by hiring a migrant domestic worker.

Of course, hiring domestic labor is a global phenomenon and occurs in most countries, with differing norms and expectations. For example, middle-class families in the U.S. hire domestic workers who generally do not live in the home, as opposed to Southeast Asian employers who generally are expected to provide a small space in the home for the domestic worker to live in, particularly if the domestic worker comes from another country. Even in the Philippines, it is not uncommon for domestic workers who have saved enough from their work abroad to return "home" to the Philippines and employ domestic workers of their own, thereby inverting a relationship of dependence they have experienced in other countries, or even to employ a domestic worker in the Philippines to maintain the household while the migrant domestic worker is abroad. Arnado argues that "(e)mploying a domestic helper in the homeland is something that overseas domestic workers brag about to raise their demeaning status in the core and semi-peripheral nations."[18] Rhacel Parreñas cites a Filipina domestic worker in Rome, Italy, who claims:

> In the Philippines, I have maids. When I came here, I kept on thinking that in the Philippines, I have maids and here I am one. I thought to myself that once I go back to the Philippines, I will not lift my finger and I will be the signora. [Laughs.] My hands will be rested and manicured, and I will wake up at twelve o'clock noon.[19]

Clearly, the relationship of employer–domestic worker is contingent on class and not reducible to a question of gender. At the same time, the overwhelming dominance of women in the profession is testament to the enduring power of patriarchy in assigning particular forms of employment on a gendered basis. Whether it is a white middle-class woman in the U.S. hiring an immigrant domestic worker or a migrant Filipina domestic worker hiring a domestic worker of her own in the Philippines, class and gender are vital to an understanding of this form of employment.

But is that enough? For most migrant domestic workers it is also imperative to interrogate the conditions of employment. Throughout this book we emphasize the importance of understanding capitalism as a form of social organization and mode of production. One of the important characteristics of capitalism, we argue, is the "freedom" that inheres in the wage relation. That is to say, as an employee you voluntarily enter into a wage relationship, and you can terminate that particular relationship by finding employment elsewhere. We stress that while the structural relationship of class compels those who do not own means of production to sell their labor to survive, capitalism's "dual freedom" means that there is scope for some choice in the wage relationship. Migrant domestic workers, and in fact most temporary migrants, are denied this freedom. When a migrant worker leaves the home country (through legal channels), a contract is signed that requires the worker to perform certain duties for a specified period of time (often two years in the case of domestic workers). The receiving country issues a visa allowing the migrant worker to work under the conditions of the contract, and should the contract be abrogated by either side, requires the migrant worker to leave the country within a short period of time and prohibits other forms of employment.

Therefore, migrant labor, under conditions of contract, is best conceived as a form of "unfree labor." Under normal conditions an employee can choose to seek other forms of employment if the conditions of work become intolerable. Of course, the employee must seek other forms of employment, and market conditions will have a lot to do with making such a decision. However, each employer is aware that an employee could choose to seek work elsewhere, or perhaps organize a union to force better conditions, or threaten to withhold labor until conditions improve. This awareness serves as an incentive, however small, to the employer to maintain workplace conditions that approximate employment conditions elsewhere in the market. The employers of contract workers *have no such incentive.* The contract serves as a tool that effectively removes one of the most important "freedoms" from the wage relation. In effect, contract migrant workers are engaged in a quasi-feudal relationship.

The feudal nature of this relationship manifests itself in the conditions women work under. Though conditions vary remarkably across and even within countries, contract domestic workers are typically provided with room and board and a modest salary. Depending on the host country, they are generally provided one day off per week, but this commitment is not always honored. Frequent reports of physical and sexual assault, combined with the withholding of wages, unpaid overtime, demands for work outside the home (such as helping in an employer's business), and paternalistic surveillance by the employer, all suggest that working conditions for migrant domestic workers are very difficult indeed. We can also add the emotional pain that accompanies being away from children, friends, and family for years at a time. With all of this to look forward to, why do so many women choose to migrate for low-paid domestic work?

A short answer is that many women claim they are "forced migrants." Particularly common among migrant women and advocacy groups that are more politically aware of the determinants of the "maid trade," the notion of "forced migration" refers to the lack of opportunity in the home country combined with government promotion of contract migration. Particularly salient for the Philippines, it is an open question whether relying so heavily on migration promotes or hinders development. If the best chance for a better life is overseas, particularly for skilled workers, there is every reason to believe that the human capital on which development is dependent will not be available. Even if we take the Philippines government at its word and accept that the promotion of migration is intended to develop external finance for development, how can a government that is dependent on remittances ever slow down the export of skilled labor? The Philippines seems to be caught on a treadmill, exporting workers to generate remittances, unable to stop to take the next step.

Arguments about forced migration aside, there are other reasons women seem eager to take up this work. One obvious factor is the relatively higher wages obtainable by working abroad. Wherever the worker is coming from, the possibility of contributing much more to the family and their own life prospects by going abroad must be tempting. Add to this the tendency for returning migrants to accentuate the positive aspect of their experience, as well as the higher status that returning migrants often experience, and it becomes clear that there are many incentives to work abroad. Finally, it must be emphasized that domestic work abroad, for all its difficulties, allows women the opportunity to experience life away from the discipline and surveillance of fathers, husbands, boyfriends, and extended family (though many must submit to the discipline and surveillance of the employer), the opportunity to control their wages (however meager), and the opportunity to experience life in another country. All of these things can produce quite contradictory responses from women who often experience ambivalent feelings about return.[20] This seemingly contradictory experience is in fact a common story among women in LDCs who encounter wage labor as young women in EPZs (on which see chapter 2).

Though contemporary evidence is mixed, EPZ employment has been composed predominantly of young women. For demanding assembly line work, women are seen as better employees than men for a variety of reasons—some outrageous, some plausible. Women are seen as less likely to organize, more docile, and more likely to work for lower wages. Reasons that this may be the case are the limited (or nonexistent) experience these women have had with wage work (as opposed to work in the household), the strong effects of patriarchal social relations, and the frequent dependence on wage income to support a family. Less plausible but frequently cited by management and host countries are the "nimble fingers" or manual dexterity of women and their putative ability to endure longer hours under difficult conditions. A Malaysian government advertisement enticing firms to an EPZ is illustrative:

> The manual dexterity of the oriental female is famous the world over. Her hands are small and she works fast with extreme care. Who, therefore, could be better qualified by nature and inheritance to contribute to the efficiency of a bench-assembly production line than the oriental girl?[21]

Of course, such cultural reasoning is adapted to the locale of the EPZ. A strikingly similar enticing investment in El Salvador advertised the low wages needed to hire women like "Rosa Martinez." The ad continues, "Rosa is more than just colorful. She and her co-workers are known for their industriousness, reliability, and quick-learning."[22] It seems the common factor in a high-quality workforce is women who will work for low wages. As disturbing as such characterizations of women are, they seem to be a prevalent feature of both host country and management attitudes.[23]

As discussed in chapter 2, the growing liberalization of trade, reductions in transportation and communication costs, and growth of transnational production chains are all aspects of contemporary globalization that have spurred the growth of EPZs and the enormous increase of women involved in wage work (often for the first time). Women in EPZs, and in low-wage manufacturing and assembly production more generally, suffer from real abuses. They are often tested for pregnancy to reduce the chance that an employee will miss work or leave the firm responsible for maternity benefits. They are forced to take contraceptives or to show evidence of menstruation.[24] Sexual harassment and physical abuse are depressingly frequent. The litany of abuses that are familiar to low-wage manufacturing, such as forced overtime, unpredictable shifts, speed-ups, dangerous working conditions, and infrequent breaks, are all prevalent in these production sites, with the added burden that women are often expected to take such abuse with much less resistance than men. However, moving from household work to wage labor has some progressive consequences, which in no way diminishes the abuses cited above.

While the outrageous abuse many EPZ workers are subjected to is now well documented, there is a need to recognize the contradictory effects such employment practices produce. As discussed in chapter 1, Marx's notion of "freedom in the dual sense" enables us to recognize these contradictory effects as the dialectical logic of capitalism—at once progressive and exploitative, creating new possibilities while simultaneously limiting, distorting, or denying their full expression. Women wage earners are provided with admittedly meager wages, but often this is the first time that such discretionary income has been available to them. Working allows these women to recognize they have value outside of traditional roles and provides them with the opportunity to spend considerable time with women their own age living in similar conditions. Further, women who move from agrarian environs to cities or export enclaves have a small but nonetheless significant amount of time available to them when not working—time that is not supervised by men. All of these effects can produce changes in the role women envision for themselves, and for mothers, the role they envision for their children. Other analyses of women in EPZs and low-wage manufacturing and assembly in LDCs have come to similar conclusions about the contradictory effects of wage labor—a kind of simultaneous oppressive/progressive combination of effects.[25]

We should expect that women who migrate for domestic work would undergo similar changes, even though the conditions of their work are different than those in low-wage manufacturing. In some ways domestic workers are under more surveillance, have less time to socialize with other women, and are arguably being reinforced into a gendered role of caregiver and housekeeper. However, they do this work for a wage, and perhaps more important, do this work in an entirely different country. Ethnographic work by Chin (1998), Constable (1997, 2002), and Parreñas (2001)[26] suggests that many of these changes do indeed occur, but at a higher cost than is the case for women engaged in low-wage production. As Constable has suggested, notions of "home" and place become scrambled in this kind of work, and for many Filipinas at least, "home" becomes an elusive, flexible concept.[27]

So, how does intersectional politics speak to efforts at resisting and redefining this form of work? How can we think about social identities that involve such complicated and contradictory determinants as class, gender, and nationality? Examining the manner in which migrant domestic workers have come together to challenge their conditions of employment may provide some clues. Given space limitations and the number of sending and receiving countries, we cannot provide an exhaustive survey of domestic workers' struggles. However, we can briefly examine the actions of migrant domestic workers in Hong Kong as an important example of these forms of struggles.

The overwhelming majority of domestic workers in Hong Kong are Filipina but, as demonstrated in table 4.2, the number of Indonesian domestic workers is growing at a rapid rate, whereas the number of Filipinas has leveled off. This is partially the result of a concerted attempt by Indonesian policy makers to cultivate remittance income as well as the two-tier nature of domestic work in Hong Kong today. Filipinas are generally better organized and aware of their rights under Hong Kong law. Indonesians are much more likely to be subjected to wages below the minimum allowed by law as well as to be taken advantage of by employers and employee placement agencies. Though there is a minimum wage of 3,270 HKD/month (approximately $420), surveys suggest that anywhere from 50 to 70 percent of Indonesians are illegally underpaid, some substantially.[28] Indonesians tend to come to Hong Kong through placement agencies in Indonesia where they are "trained" with rudimentary Cantonese and the use of household appliances common in Hong Kong. For this service Indonesian domestic workers are frequently required to pay several months' wages as "reimbursement" for their "education," as opposed to other na-

Table 4.2   Foreign Domestic Workers in Hong Kong

Year	Philippines	Indonesia	Thailand	Other	Total
1990	63,600	1,000	4,300	1,400	70,300
1991	75,700	1,800	5,600	1,500	84,600
1992	89,100	3,500	6,700	1,900	101,200
1993	105,400	6,100	7,000	2,100	120,600
1994	121,200	10,700	7,100	2,400	141,400
1995	131,200	16,400	6,700	2,700	157,000
1996	134,700	21,000	5,800	2,800	164,300
1997	138,100	24,700	5,100	3,100	171,000
1998	140,500	31,800	5,300	3,000	180,600
1999	143,200	41,400	5,760	3,340	193,700
2000	151,490	55,200	6,450	3,650	216,790
2001	155,450	68,880	7,000	3,950	235,280
2002	148,390	78,170	6,670	3,880	237,110

Source: Hong Kong Department of Immigration, personal communication with labor attaché, 2003.

tionalities, which usually pay a placement fee before entering Hong Kong. Indonesians are more likely to work in Chinese households, while Filipinas, often better educated and able to speak English well, are more likely to work for European or American expatriates (though there is considerable Filipina employment within Chinese households as well).

Filipina domestic workers in Hong Kong have successfully organized to resist several government attempts to change the conditions of employment for domestic workers. In 1999 and 2001 wage cuts were fought back, and in 2000 the attempted removal of maternity protection was resisted, with appeals to media outlets, street rallies, protests, and candlelight vigils.[29] Since the introduction of migrant domestic workers in 1974, Filipinas have slowly organized into unions that have acquired substantial memberships. Unions like United Filipinos (UNIFIL) and Filipino Migrant Workers' Union (FMWU) have been joined by advocacy organizations and NGOs like Asian Migrant Centre (AMC) and Mission for Filipino Migrant Workers (MFMW). There are also coordinating bodies that seek to unite different nationalities around common advocacy themes. Filipinos, whether domestic workers or other migrant workers, have been the most organized and effective in realizing a collective (if at times fractious) voice.[30] Other nationalities are far behind the Filipinos in terms of organization, but serious efforts are being made, and recent unions include Indonesian Migrant Workers' Union (IMWU), Thai Women's Association (TWA), and umbrella groups like Asian Domestic Workers' Union (ADWU).

Earlier government proposals to reduce domestic workers' wages have been fought back by domestic worker groups. However, demonstrations and media actions were unable to prevent the Hong Kong government's successful passage of a 400 HKD per month wage cut in 2003.[31] The Hong Kong government argued that the wage cut was necessary for budgetary deficit reduction as well as the training of local domestic workers so as to provide employment opportunities for Hong Kong citizens. Given the government deficit at the time as well as the general economic crisis in Hong Kong, it is difficult not to view the wage cut as a kind of scapegoating. Much of the public commentary about these issues was drowned out in the SARS crisis, which also occurred in the first half of 2003.

Though domestic workers in Hong Kong are represented by a number of unions, they have never gone on strike, and there remains disagreement among domestic workers about the strategy of unionizing. Some have suggested that the failure to stop the 2003 wage cut demonstrates that unions are ineffective, while others argue that unions need to be strengthened to the point of effectively threatening a strike. Among the many challenges faced by domestic workers in these campaigns are the short stay of some domestic workers (as little as two years); the necessity of leaders to work six days a week and organize in their limited free time; and the difficulty in coordinating among a large number of unions, advocacy groups, and NGOs. In addition, the linguistic and cultural challenges of working across national boundaries should not be overlooked. Though domestic workers have exhibited real solidarity across national lines in the past, the increasing number of Indonesian domestic workers and the unwillingness of the Indonesian consulate to make a strong stand against the proposal have been pointed to as reasons the government was able to pass the wage cut. One NGO director in Hong Kong suggested that the cooperation the POEA has extended to other countries is precisely driven by the desire to present a collective front to host governments in the future.

In researching the material for this chapter, one of us (Solomon) was able to interview a number of Filipina and Indonesian domestic workers in Hong Kong involved in advocacy work for migrants. Though we cannot rule out the possibility that domestic workers involved in advocacy work and union organizing have opinions that are outside the mainstream beliefs of domestic workers in Hong Kong, their self-understandings were illustrative of the degree to which these processes are integrated within globalization and understood as such.

The primary questions for interview subjects related to how they viewed their situation relative to state policies of the sending country, their remittances, and their position within a global economy. When Filipinas were asked how they felt about being considered "heroes of the nation," they generally mocked the entire notion, seeing it as a cynical attempt to increase remittance income. Though not every Filipina interviewed mocked this discourse, no one embraced the concept or felt she was furthering economic development in the Philippines.[32] When one Indonesian was asked about the government's attempt to increase domestic worker outflows, she summarized her understanding of government policy as, "If you sell a banana you only profit once, if you sell a person you keep getting profit while they are overseas." Every domestic worker interviewed felt that her government benefited from her working abroad, generally expressed in the logic of remittance income to the state. The IMWU (recently formed and one of the first Indonesian unions) has produced a documentary VCD entitled *2.5 Billion Dollar[s] for the State* (its estimate of the total remittance income generated annually by migrant workers). Clearly, the logic of remittance income seems clear to domestic workers in Hong Kong.

Not surprisingly, many of the women interviewed viewed themselves as "commodities," "things," or "products" that were bought and sold. This may be more pronounced among domestic workers in Hong Kong given its role as a global and financial center, but it is telling that this terminology is used for the person. They did not view themselves as only providing a service but as a good that crosses borders and therefore is like any other commodity that is traded. This may be reinforced by the sense that there is a market for their services that varies with location and other conditions.

Given these self-understandings, it is clearly not much of a jump for these women to understand the process they represent as indicative of globalization. However, when globalization was invoked it was generally used to mean "more trade" and "more people crossing borders." Though "neoliberal globalization" was mentioned by many workers, both Filipina and Indonesian, as something they were opposed to, it was not clear what exactly this meant to them other than a shorthand for the remittance-driven policies of their sending countries. While our analysis in preceding chapters suggests that there is some validity to this kind of claim, it is not clear from the conversations with migrant domestic workers that "neoliberal globalization" meant much more to them than "globalization" more generally.

Perhaps most surprising was the continued use of the term "forced migration" to describe their situation. Domestic workers were very clear and nearly unanimous about this. Though they had short-term goals of improving the conditions of their employment, the long-term goal was that their states reshape their economic development policies to allow for sustainable employment in the home economy. We found this surprising given that these women, at some level, did make a choice to emigrate abroad for employment. No doubt the notion of "forced migration" would not be as strong among a larger sample of domestic workers, but one would also expect to hear more of this explanation as countries like Indonesia and the Philippines seek to further the export of contract migrants.

For a better understanding of why and how Filipina domestic workers can think of themselves as wrapped up in circuits of globalization, it is important to note a watershed moment in OFW resistance to the Philippine state's instrumental use of migrants. In 1995 a Filipina domestic worker in Singapore, Flor Contemplacion, was hanged by the Singapore government for the murder of a fellow domestic worker and the employer's child. Although the facts of the case were contested, the inability of the Philippine government to stop the execution served as a symbolic representation of how powerless the Philippine state was in protecting millions of overseas Filipinos. The response among Filipinos was global, igniting protests and mobilizing "opposition parties, church associations, women's groups, labor unions" and other OFW organizations.[33] Massive pressure at home and abroad forced the Philippine legislature to pass the watershed Republic Act 8042, commonly known as the Migrant Workers and Overseas Filipinos Act of 1995.[34] Though the act called for a variety of strengthened protections for migrant workers, the weakness of the Philippine state vis-à-vis labor receiving states has prevented much in the way of concrete achievements. What made the act so significant for OFWs was the ability of migrants and their allies to pressure the state into action.[35] Not only were administrative changes made, the Philippine state publicly acknowledged that the welfare and rights of workers were to be a primary concern, not merely the satisfaction of economic goals. As Castles and Miller observe, the 1995 Act was a sort of "Magna Carta" for OFWs.[36] We would go further and argue that the 1995 Act was a public acknowledgment that the Philippine state was increasingly composed of a global polity, and that the deterritorialization of the Philippine state was being codified. As the quote at the beginning of this chapter demonstrates, politicians and policy makers in the Philippines must increasingly pay attention to constituents around the world. The frequently cited number of eight million overseas Filipinos masks the much larger impact on the Philippines, as each of these eight million Filipinos has family and friends at home who either rely on remittance income or at least are concerned with the well-being of OFWs.

So what does *deterritorialization* really mean, beyond having a bunch of citizens living overseas? Traditionally, states have been conceived as territorially exclusive "containers" within which the state has complete sovereignty.[37] Sovereignty was thought of as mutually exclusive so that all territory (literally, all land and parts of the seas and airspace) was divided up among different states, and each state was the exclusive authority within its boundaries. For the purposes of political theory and practical politics, the people who reside within a state, the citizenry, have been conceived as carrying out their economic and political life within the state. In chapter 2 we discuss how capitalism has structural characteristics that result in economic activity increasingly taking place across state borders. For the Philippines, *formal political activity* is increasingly taking place outside of the state. Especially for democracies, "the people" is the foundation for the state's appeal to legitimacy. What happens when large portions of the citizenry are outside of the state's borders? We argue that in the case of the Philippines, deterritorialization is the result. This is not an argument that the territory disappears, but rather that significant elements of the political and economic processes traditionally conceived as coterminous with state territory are happening outside of the state. Thus, the Philippine state is best conceived of as increasingly deterritorialized.

The codification of this deterritorialization was furthered by some recent changes to voting and citizenship laws in the Philippines. In February 2003 the Absentee Voting Bill was passed into law, followed by the Dual Citizenship Bill, which was signed in August 2003. The Absentee Voting Bill was the culmination of a long grassroots struggle by migrant worker advocacy networks to allow an electoral voice for the now nearly eight million Filipinos living and working abroad. The voting law allows for migrants abroad to register and vote in national elections and for the "party-list" system (a complicated proportional voting system that allots 20 percent of the seats in the lower house). The first test of the new law was the national presidential and legislative elections of May 2004. In terms of migrant worker political strength, the results of the election were mixed. According to the Commission on Elections of the Philippines (COMELEC), only about 360,000 overseas Filipinos registered to vote in the elections. This is certainly below the figure many had hoped for. However, many have suggested that the hurdles required for registration and voting, such as an OFW in Norway being required to travel to Stockholm to register and then again to vote, certainly suppressed voting, as did the unfamiliarity of the new process. Indicative of the global reach of the process was the number of countries that had OFWs who voted. Nearly eighty different countries had Filipinos who voted while overseas and ran the gamut from large concentrations in Saudi Arabia (96,876), Hong Kong (88,001), and Singapore (23,949), to smaller numbers in unexpected places like Chile (57), Romania (36), and Senegal (with a single voter). Though disaggregated numbers have not been released, and we cannot ascertain if overseas votes made any real difference in the party list candidates, some gains are undeniable. The global nature of campaigning for party-list candidates through rallies, print media, and the Internet, as well as the willingness of 360,000 overseas Filipinos to deal with the bureaucratic hassle of registering and voting in their very limited free time (for some involving personal expense and travel), demonstrates that many OFWs seek to make claims on the state through the ballot and other means. Assuming that voting is made easier for OFWs (through pressure on the government), there is every reason to believe that OFWs can become a significant political force, perhaps matching their economic contribution.

The Dual Citizenship Bill allows Filipinos to have dual citizenship with other countries (as long as they are not serving in the military of another country or holding office of another country). The bill is essentially an acknowledgment of the capital and skills that many Filipinos have acquired abroad. The Philippine state is seeking to solicit capital and skills from those who have emigrated and secured citizenship elsewhere (primarily the U.S., Canada, and Western Europe). The hope is that by providing dual citizenship overseas Filipinos will feel more connection to the Philippines, investment will be encouraged, and new economic networks will be created and sustained. Of course, it also provides a de jure recognition of a de facto reality—the drain of skilled workers from the Philippines and the difficulty of economic development without them. Obviously, this is one more example of how the Philippines is steadily codifying the increasingly deterritorialized nature of its polity, economy, and state.

Conclusion

We have spent a considerable amount of time discussing the Philippines, the paradigmatic example of a labor-exporting state. Space constraints keep us from having a comparable discussion about similar cases such as Indonesia, Sri Lanka, or Bangladesh. Obviously, other countries have massive migrant flows as well but differ from this case because the state is less involved in encouraging migration or migrants are oriented toward permanent settlement if possible. Mexico is a good example of such a country. Millions of Mexicans have migrated to the U.S., pushed by difficult economic circumstances at home and pulled by the steady supply of employment in construction, agriculture, and other industries (which would be devastated if this source of cheap labor were effectively stopped). While the long-ruling Mexican Partido Revolucionario Institucional (PRI) largely ignored the role of migrants until the 1990s and even considered them "traitors" at times, the Vicente Fox administration that came to power in 2000 ended seven decades of one-party rule and inaugurated a new era of state policy on migration. President Fox, echoing policy makers in the Philippines, has consistently referred to Mexican migrants as "heroes" and has sought to redefine the immigration question with the U.S. (largely derailed after 9/11). In another echo of the Philippines, one migration scholar claims President Fox sees emigrants "as heroes who were forced to leave their country and nevertheless contributed $12 billion to its economy in 2002."[38] Given the rhetoric of recognition Fox has utilized toward migrants, it is not surprising that in June 2004 he sent a bill to the Mexican legislature that would allow absentee voting for president by Mexicans in the U.S. (*Economist*, June 24, 2004). Though all three major Mexican political parties (PRI, Partido Acción Nacional [PAN], and Partido de la Revolución Democrática [PRD]) agree to the concept, the many logistical, financial, and political hurdles the bill faces make its future uncertain, especially for the 2006 elections. Nevertheless, Mexico, like the Philippines and other states with a sizable migrant population, is struggling with ways to maintain the concept of democratic legitimacy with a large measure of its polity outside its borders.

Similar to the argument we make in chapter 3, we believe the possibilities of transnational solidarity are expressed in the struggles around migration but in differing ways. Much of our discussion in previous chapters takes up processes that involve transnational capital calling into being a transnational politics rooted in particular communities—some geographically defined, some better conceived as communities of interest. Uniting all of these struggles is a "dialectic of power" wherein inequalities of wealth and power produce an ongoing contestation of the contours, circuits, and possibilities of contemporary globalization. We have suggested that one product of the process of migration is a contestation and redefinition of particular states, polities, and economies. With respect to the Philippines, and perhaps increasingly to other states, we argue that we are witnessing the deterritorialization of the state. Much of this process has been forced by grassroots pressure from organized migrants and advocacy groups. Other elements have been the product of state policy makers grappling with a process created, but certainly not controlled, by the state. As we have consistently argued, capitalism's dialectical process of "dual freedom" simultaneously produces freedom and unfreedom, opening some possibilities while closing others off.

As migration volumes increase, and they surely will in the short term whether driven by state policy or the push-pull forces of capitalist globalization, the growing number of migrants creates certain possibilities. One end of a spectrum of possibilities would be a new politics of "flexible citizenship" wherein increasing numbers of people begin to master multiple political, economic, and cultural logics; nationalism erodes as citizenship becomes more complex; and a new politics of democracy rethinks the boundaries that have kept democratic practice so impoverished.[39] The other end of that spectrum is obvious and frighteningly present in some manifestations alluded to above. From J. M. Le Pen and Patrick Buchanan to the latest work of Samuel Huntington, the possibility of varying degrees of nativist reaction is depressingly common. Add to this the terrorist attacks of September 11, 2001, and the jingoistic, hypernationalist response of the Bush administration (you're either with us or against us), and the groundwork is laid for ever more base appeals to fear and a politics of "us and them." Any study of contemporary globalization would be incomplete without an analysis of what the "war on terror" and the inexplicable inclusion of the invasion of Iraq portend for the global political economy. We next turn to that question, and consistent with our understanding of HM, argue that although much is different about the world after 9/11, a full understanding of this conflict requires a recognition of the continuities that persist.

GLOBALIZATION, IMPERIALISM, AND TERROR

Since the spectacular and horrible attacks of September 2001, the politics of globalization may seem to have dramatically veered off course, with the terms of global debate and political contestation shifting as the world's most powerful state apparently changed its emphasis from the institutionalization of global economic integration to a policy of global military supremacy pursued under the banner of the "war on terror." We argue in this chapter that although the policies of the second Bush administration have indeed represented significant shifts in the means of U.S. global strategy, there remain underlying continuities between these policies and the longstanding U.S. strategic goal of the promotion of liberal capitalism on a global scale. That terror and the war on terror may have dominated global political discourse in recent years does not mean that struggles surrounding globalization have been eclipsed, that these debates are no longer relevant. Rather, we claim, globalization, imperialism, terror, and war are aspects of a complex and ongoing tale of global politics.

We wish to argue not that terrorism has been "caused" by imperialism and globalization in any simple or immediate sense—much less that these in any way justify mass murder—but that imperialism and globalization are crucial aspects of the context in which terrorism has arisen, and that the emergence of terrorism cannot be fully understood without some sense of this historical context. Further, the U.S. "war on terror" has direct continuities with this history of imperialism and globalization—a history that is itself not innocent of mass murder.[1] Although Americans tend to overlook them, these continuities are not lost on the great bulk of the world's people and underlie the contemporary explosion of anti-American sentiment worldwide. From our perspective, then, imperialism, terrorism, and the "war on terror" are bound up with the politics of globalization and the history of capitalism. We sketch out our view of that nexus below.

9/11 and Global Structural Privilege

Most Americans were stunned and bewildered by the attacks of September 11. With little or no awareness of their contextual relation to the U.S. global role, many saw the attacks as not just unjustifiable, but inexplicable. There was in this context much talk of "lost innocence" and how "everything has changed." In our view, what changed after September 11—in ways profoundly disturbing and threatening to Americans—was the sense that their lives were lived in a separate social space, uniquely privileged, largely immune to the troubles that plague much of the rest of the world. What was lost, then, was the comfort and security afforded by the assurance—itself an unacknowledged effect of global structural power—that "those things don't happen here"—a telling comment, expressed in tones of deep shock, heard often in the wake of the attacks. This, we believe, is what lies behind Americans' traumatized sense that they now live in a changed world; the world may not itself have changed, but Americans' perception of the ways in which they live in that world surely had.

This realization might have led to a questioning of America's role in producing and sustaining a world of inequality, of violence both overt and structural. "Structural violence" refers to the harmful social effects of massive inequality, a social structure in which concentrations of great wealth and fabulous luxury coexist with extensive squalor and billions of people whose basic needs are unmet, and in which these inequalities are upheld by concentrations of social and political power. In light of available evidence, there is every reason to believe that the world produced by contemporary globalization is permeated by such structural violence. According to United Nations data (see table 2.2), the modern world has become increasingly unequal over the last two centuries, with this inequality becoming much more (rather than less) marked as globalization has accelerated under U.S. leadership in recent decades. And residents of the U.S. *benefit disproportionately* from this structured inequality. While Americans represent only about 5 *percent* of the entire world's population, they enjoy nearly 30 *percent* of the world's income. Further, the U.S. receives over a quarter of the world's total inflows of direct foreign investment; accounts for over 22 percent of the world's energy consumption; generates nearly a quarter of the world's total emissions of carbon dioxide; and owns about 27 percent of the world's telephone lines, mobile phones, and personal computers. Taken together, such indicators of disproportionate material wealth suggest that the life chances enjoyed by persons who live in the U.S. are substantially better than those of most of the rest of the world's people, and indeed the average life expectancy of an American is about 116 percent of the world average.[2] Of course, the benefits of global structural privilege accrue most dramatically to the richest Americans: "The richest 10% of the US population has an income equal to that of the poorest 43% of the world. Put differently, the income of the richest 25 million Americans is equal to that of almost 2 billion people."[3] Notwithstanding such class-based differentials among Americans, however, the structural violence of globalizing capitalism means that U.S. citizens in general live richer and longer lives than the great bulk of the world's people.

So the attacks of 9/11 might have prompted some reflection on the ways in which globalization's structural violence benefits Americans, the resentments that this engenders worldwide, and whether such global conditions are conducive to peace and security. But such questioning would have entailed moving away from collective self-understandings based on American exceptionalism,[4] and an explicit acknowledgment of structural positioning based on economic and political power and privilege, and this most Americans are not (yet?) prepared to do. Instead, the shock of the terrorist attacks gave way to strident reassertions of American exceptionalism and privilege, a hyperpatriotism profoundly suspicious of otherness, and a blatantly neoimperial foreign policy sold to Americans on the grounds that aggressive exercise of U.S. military power could protect them from future terrorist attacks while implicitly preserving their position of (global structural) privilege. In its effort to shape the consent of the American public for its war plans, the Bush administration framed 9/11 and the ensuing "war on terror" in terms of a self-righteous, Manichean moralism. This is clearly evident in Bush's rhetoric: "You've probably learned by now, I don't believe there's many shades of gray in this war. You're either with us or against us. You're either evil, or you're good."[5] Perhaps ironically, such rhetoric mirrors the moral absolutism of the fundamentalist Islamists whom Bush opposes. Declarations such as Bush's clearly presupposed the moral purity of the U.S. and implied that any country or person not fully compliant with U.S. policy was effectively in league with terrorists. To the extent that this ideological strategy has been successful, Americans tend to view current events in abstraction from America's history of imperialism and its intimate connection to U.S. global privilege and are likely to see the reassertion of U.S. military power as a purely defensive move, a response to unprovoked and unjustifiable terrorist attacks perpetrated by "evil-doers" whose only conceivable motivation is that "they hate our freedom."

However, the imperial exercise of coercive force pervades the history of U.S. foreign policy. From its colonial origin to its role in reshaping the twentieth-century capitalist world order, the U.S. has been intimately involved with imperial power: the forceful expropriation and near extermination of native Americans; military conquest and absorption of substantial territories formerly belonging to Mexico; establishing domination of the hemisphere and enforcing capitalist property rights on a transnational scale through enactment of the Monroe Doctrine and the Roosevelt corollary; annexation of Hawaii and conquest of Cuba, Puerto Rico, the Philippines, and other territories used as strategic bases in the pursuit of an "Open Door" for U.S. capital seeking to expand its sphere of operations; twentieth-century global order struggles leading to the destruction of fascism—with its political economy of militarized autarky—and the subsequent reconstruction of the infrastructure of the capitalist world economy; and the "containment" of a putative global communist threat that was invoked to justify numerous bloody interventions both overt and covert to secure the "free world"—understood as a hospitable environment for U.S. political and economic interests—during the second half of the twentieth century.[6] Such exercises of imperial power were (to put it mildly) not always consistent with professed values of human rights and democracy.

Global Power, Fordist Capitalism, and the Politics of Oil

Petroleum emerged as a strategic commodity singularly important for global politics during the first half of the twentieth century. Initially, its significance derived from its military utility, especially in the global projection of naval power. In the early years of the century, when Britain's global naval preeminence was being challenged by Germany's construction of a substantial fleet of warships, Lord of the Admiralty Winston Churchill summarized what seemed to be at stake for Britain: "The whole fortunes of our race and Empire, the whole treasure accumulated during so many centuries of sacrifice and achievement, would perish and be swept utterly away if our naval supremacy were to be impaired."[7] It was in this context that oil-powered warships were found to have decisive advantages of range, speed, and flexibility over coal-fired fleets, and the British Royal Navy set new standards of naval capability when it began building a more powerful, faster, oil-powered fleet before World War I.[8] Since Britain sat on great islands of coal but possessed at that time no significant oil resources, this decision entailed a long-term strategic commitment to maintain British influence in those regions of the world where supplies of oil sufficient to power the Royal Navy could be secured, primarily in the Middle East (a region also deemed crucial for British imperial power due to the Suez Canal and the sea lanes it connected from Britain to India). The primary instrument of Britain's global petro-politics was the Anglo-Persian Oil company (later British Petroleum), which held oil concessions in Iran deemed so significant that the British government bought a majority stake in the company to ensure its control of Iranian oil and guarantee preferential access for the Royal Navy.[9]

After World War I, Middle Eastern oil outside of Persia was dominated by major firms from Britain, Holland, France, and the U.S. through a series of agreements. The most significant of these was the Red Line Agreement of 1928, in which a consortium of major oil companies—collectively known as the Iraq Petroleum Company—agreed jointly to exploit the oil resources within the territory of the former Ottoman Empire stretching from Turkey to the tip of the Arabian peninsula. Under the terms of the agreement, Anglo-Persian and Royal Dutch /Shell together were to receive almost 50 percent of the oil jointly exploited within that territory, while French and American firms each held rights to just under one-quarter.[10] This arrangement shaped imperial domination of the region until British influence was displaced by that of the U.S. after World War II.

With the development of mechanized warfare during World War II, mass-produced armadas of oil-powered military machines—on land and in the air as well as at sea—proved indispensable to victory. Direct access to American oil, supplies of which were at that time relatively plentiful, and the denial of similarly abundant supplies to Germany and Japan, was a crucial factor underlying the Allied victory in that global struggle.[11] By the mid-twentieth century, the strategic importance of petroleum was beyond question; effective global power clearly required reliable access to enormous supplies of oil to fuel the projection of massive military force over sea, air, and land, and the ability to deny such access to rivals had been shown to be a decisive strategic instrument.

In addition to oil's military significance, Fordist capitalism depended on oil as fuel for internal combustion engines in automobiles, trucks and tractors, airplanes, and ships; as a lubricant for machines of all sorts; and as a necessary raw material for the petrochemical industry. All of this was essential not just for Fordist industry but also for ever more capital- and chemical-intensive agriculture. Cheap and plentiful oil made possible the construction of "increasingly industrialized and urbanized society which involved the suburbanization of cities, the switch from public to private transport, the mechanization of housework and better standards of heating."[12] In short, oil was becoming indispensable to the energy-intensive form of Fordist capitalism that the U.S. sought to reconstruct as the core of the postwar world economy.

American global strategy after World War II was aimed not just at "containing" the power of the Soviet Union but also at creating a world that would be hospitable to the growth of American-centered capitalism. Widely regarded as a foundational document of U.S. postwar world order strategy, National Security Council Document 68 (NSC-68) called on the U.S. to assume a role of "world leadership" "to create conditions under which our free and democratic system can live and prosper."[13] The "free and democratic system" that U.S. leaders wanted to promote and protect worldwide was axiomatically identified with capitalism. U.S. strategists explicitly envisioned a symbiotic relationship between the vitality and robustness of the capitalist "free world"—in their words, "an international economy based on multilateral trade, declining trade barriers, and convertible currencies"—and globally projected U.S. military power capable of defending "any of several vital pressure points" where the "free world" might be vulnerable to incursion or subversion.[14] In a polarized, zero-sum world where "a defeat of free institutions anywhere is a defeat everywhere," U.S. national security and the survival of "civilization itself" was thus seen to depend on a liberalized and reinvigorated world capitalism and the possession of "clearly superior overall power" by the U.S. and its "free world" allies.[15] Viewed through the lense of this strategic vision, protecting the "free world" was closely identified with promoting a vigorous U.S.-centered capitalist world economy, and it was this worldview that appeared to justify U.S. interventions to counter political forces—even if not directly related to the U.S.S.R.—that might inhibit the growth of American-dominated global capitalism. Though the relative balance between coercive and consensual aspects of U.S. global domination may have shifted from one historical conjuncture to another, variants of this basic strategy governed U.S. world order policy throughout the Cold War period.

The U.S. strategic goal of establishing a postwar hegemonic world order required rebuilding Europe and Japan along Fordist lines as industrial bulwarks of the capitalist "free world," and since U.S. oil supplies were finite while global demand was not, this too had crucial implications for global petro-politics.

> Although U.S. oil provided nearly six-sevenths of allied oil during the war, it was clear that future supplies to Western Europe . . . and Japan would have to come primarily from the Middle East. Indeed, [postwar] US hegemony depended on rapid and stable growth in these areas, and in turn this depended on plentiful supplies of cheap oil. US control over the international oil industry was therefore seen by wartime planners as a key element to their designs for the postwar order . . . . Specifically, control over Middle East oil reserves and the displacement of the erstwhile imperial power, the United Kingdom, was required in order that US possession of low-cost Middle East oil could underpin European (and Japanese) recovery.[16]

Pivotal to postwar U.S. strategic dominance in the Middle East were its relations with Iran and Saudi Arabia. U.S. influence in Iran was secured for a quarter century by the 1953 CIA-sponsored coup in which the democratically elected prime minister, Mohammad Mossadegh, was overthrown by forces who reestablished the autocratic power of the Iranian monarch, the Shah. Mossadegh was an ardent Iranian nationalist whose political movement directly challenged British control of Iran's rich oil resources by nationalizing facilities of the British-owned Anglo-Iranian Oil Company. Just as Anglo-Iranian had served as a vehicle for British domination of Iranian oil and control over the profits that flowed from it, so American firms dominated the oil industry of Saudi Arabia. Franklin Roosevelt had established a cooperative relationship with the autocratic Saudi ruling dynasty in 1945: "Roosevelt forged an agreement with Abdul-Aziz ibn Saud, the founder of the modern Saudi dynasty, to protect the royal family against its internal and external enemies in return for privileged access to Saudi oil."[17] A consortium of major U.S. oil companies named the Arabian-American Oil Company (ARAMCO) was formed between 1944 and 1948 to exploit the buried treasure of Saudi Arabia's incomparable oil fields. It is in this context that we may begin to appreciate the magnitude of the dangers actually posed by Mossadegh and the Iranian oil nationalization. Insofar as a successful Iranian nationalization might appear to peoples around the region—or indeed the world—as an example of how they could themselves reclaim control over the natural resources being exploited by dominant foreign firms, this was a strategic threat to Anglo-American control over the increasingly important oil reserves of the Persian Gulf region, and perhaps even Western access to Third World resources more generally. Mossadegh was painted in the West as a communist sympathizer and menace to the capitalist "free world," and Cold War strategic rivalry was invoked as the rationale for his removal. After a false start, American and British intelligence agencies ultimately engineered a successful coup, and Mossadegh's elected government was replaced by the militaristic and repressive—if also reliably pro-American—regime of Mohammad Reza Shah. In the wake of the coup Iran's oil concessions were renegotiated, with British and American firms now equally sharing control. Meanwhile, the Shah's SAVAK secret police organization—trained and equipped by U.S. military and intelligence—terrorized Iran's population; brutally repressed dissent; and enabled the Shah to impose a program of state-led, Western-oriented, secular modernization. Along with the U.S.–Saudi relationship, the Shah's Iran became a cornerstone of U.S. strategic dominance in the oil-rich Persian Gulf region. In light of this history, it is little wonder that the Iranian Revolution that finally ended the Shah's rule in 1979 fused a Shiite Islamic theocracy with bitter anti-Americanism.[18] Nor should it be surprising that the U.S.–Saudi relationship is deeply ambivalent, with widespread resentment of U.S. influence (and, for the last decade, military presence) in the kingdom finding expression through the fundamentalist Wahhabi brand of Sunni Islam that predominates there.

With the end of the Cold War, the coercive aspects of U.S. power were deemphasized, submerged within a discourse of spontaneous, voluntary, and generally beneficial globalization. The neoliberal triumphalism that constituted the hegemonic ideology of the post–Cold War era seemed to suggest that depoliticized market relations were natural and necessary products of human social evolution, and that with the extension of market-based liberalism and their putatively attendant republican political institutions would come a spreading zone of peace and prosperity potentially encompassing the globe. Exemplary of this perspective is Thomas Friedman, who comes as close to being an official spokesperson of the global capitalist bloc as anyone. Friedman's depictions of globalization contain a revealing contradiction: The dominant theme of his narrative suggests that global capitalism emerges spontaneously out of a universal interest in freedom, progress, and prosperity. Lurking under the surface of Friedman's story of natural and spontaneous capitalist global development, however, is a frank acknowledgment of the role of coercive force in maintaining this system: "The hidden hand of the market will never work without the hidden fist. . . . And the hidden fist that keeps the world safe for Silicon Valley's technologies to flourish is called the US Army, Air Force, Navy and Marine Corps."[19] This acknowledgment is accompanied by remarkably little reflection about *why* this is so, or what this might mean for the presumption of spontaneous and voluntary capitalist globalization, thus leaving intact the simple and happy plot line of Friedman's story: Globalization is giving the world's people what they want. This was, in effect, the official story of neoliberal capitalist globalization.[20]

While the market-oriented liberal vision continues to animate U.S. world order policy, it is no longer represented by key U.S. policy makers to be presumptively natural or spontaneous—that is, voluntary, cooperative, and multilateral—but is now portrayed more explicitly as the product of the global assertion of unilateral U.S. power, especially military force. Coercion was never absent from neoliberal capitalism, of course, but to the greatest extent possible the exercise of power underlying this system was hidden or disguised. During recent decades the most significant coercive mechanisms prying open the global South for neoliberal capitalism and (re)subjecting working people to the discipline of capital were the structural adjustment programs administered by multilateral international financial institutions, their exercise of power simultaneously mystified and legitimated by the scientific aura of neoclassical economics. Now, however, there has been a shift in the balance of coercion/consent at the core of U.S. global policy, with the unilateral and directly coercive elements officially foregrounded in ways that they have not been in recent years. The occasion for this shift involves the rise of Islamist militance in a region of the world strategically crucial for the energy-intensive global capitalism that the U.S. seeks to promote and to dominate.

Globalization, Militant Islam, and Terror

The Muslim world is vast and diverse in culture, religious practices, and politics—encompassing over a fifth of humanity distributed around the globe.[21] In recent decades there have emerged within the worldwide Muslim community (ummah) tendencies often referred to as Islamism, or political Islam, which emphasize renewed attentiveness to the fundamentals of Islamic tradition—the scriptures of the Quran, the Hadith and Sunnah or sayings and traditional practices associated with the prophet Muhammad and his closest followers, and shariah law based on these—as the comprehensive and unquestionable guide to a good life and just society. The most militant subgroups of Islamists have reinterpreted Islamic traditions and especially the injunction to religious striving and struggle, or jihad, in ways that sanctify attacks on those perceived as threatening to Islam and the ummah. These attacks have included strikes against both military and civilian targets around the world, with mass casualties, trauma, and dread as their intended result. The roots of Islamist terror are deep and tangled, and we cannot hope here to provide anything like a full account. But we try to sketch out some of the major factors identified by other scholars and some of the most important ways in which these may be related to processes of globalization.

Following on centuries of colonization and resistance, the twentieth century too was characterized by processes of globalization driven predominantly by Europe and America, and perceived in most of the world as forceful subordination to Western political and economic power and cultural mores. Much of the Middle East was effectively colonized by Britain and France when the Ottoman Empire was dismembered after World War I. Both European colonizers used brutal applications of military power (including aerial bombardment against civilian-inhabited areas) to suppress anticolonial resistance movements, but after imposing colonial nation-states that were often ill-suited to local conditions, the colonizers were eventually compelled to withdraw.[22] In the decades after World War II, hopes for Arab nationalism, economic development, and renewed international influence and respect raised popular expectations across the Arab world. But these high hopes were to be bitterly disappointed by political corruption, economic stagnation, American strategic dominance in the region, and stunning military defeats at the hands of Israel and its Western backers. It was in this context that increasingly alienated groups of devout Muslims began to rethink the meaning of Islam in the modern, Western-dominated world. John Esposito, a leading American scholar of Islam, explains:

> The causes of the [fundamentalist Islamic] resurgence vary by country and region, but there are common threads: widespread feelings of failure and loss of identity in many Muslim societies, as well as failed political systems and economies. Overcrowded cities with insufficient social support systems, high unemployment rates, government corruption, a growing gap between rich and poor, and the breakdown of traditional religious and social values plagued many nations. Israel's crushing victory over the combined forces of Egypt, Jordan, and Syria in the 1967 Arab-Israeli Six-Day War symbolized the depth of Arab and Muslim impotence and the failure of modern nation-states in the Muslim world. . . . Disillusionment with the West and in particular with the United States, its pro-Israel policy, and its support for authoritarian rulers like Iran's shah fed anti-Western feelings. Muslim religious leaders and activists believed their message had been vindicated, maintaining that the failures and troubles of Muslims were a result of turning away from God's revealed path and relying on the West. From the 1970s onward, religious revivalism and the role of Islamic movements became a major force in Muslim politics.[23]

Esposito argues that it is a mistake to view this Islamist resurgence in terms of prevalent Western stereotypes of anachronistic primitives fighting against the tide of history and progress to preserve a crude, premodern way of life: "They were neofundamentalist in the sense that they returned to the sources or fundamentals of Islam. But they reinterpreted Islamic sources in response to the challenges of the modern world. . . . Indeed, many Islamic activists are the product of modern educations, leaders in professional associations of physicians, engineers, lawyers, journalists, university professors and students."[24]

A leading example was Sayyid Qutb, an Egyptian literary scholar and educator who had traveled at length in America and been profoundly revolted by what he perceived as an immoral, materialistic, self-indulgent—and racist—culture. Opposing not just Western influence in the Islamic world but also secular Arab nationalism epitomized by the Egyptian regime of Gamal Abdel Nasser, Qutb joined the militant Muslim Brotherhood and—before his execution by the Egyptian government in 1966—became a leading intellectual of the modern Islamist revival. Reinterpreting strains of Islamic revivalist thought dating back many centuries, Qutb saw the modern Western-dominated world as analogous to the pre-Islamic era of Arab paganism—"jahiliyya," or idolatrous ignorance—against which the prophet Muhammad had struggled to reestablish the straight path of obedience to God:

> If we look at . . . modern modes of living, it becomes clear that the whole world is steeped in jahiliyya, and all the marvelous material comforts and high-level inventions do not diminish this ignorance. This jahiliyya is based on rebellion against the sovereignty of Allah on earth . . . not in the simple and primitive ways of the ancient jahiliyya, but in the more subtle form of claiming that the right to create values, to legislate rules of collective behavior, to choose a way of life rests with men, without regard to what Allah has prescribed.[25]

Here Qutb located the root of modernity's corruptions and injustices: In a world where men arrogate to themselves the power to legislate that rightfully belongs only to God, domination, exploitation, and manifold evils become embedded in man's laws, governments, and ways of living. To counter this modern jahiliyya, Qutb encouraged the most faithful of Muslims to see themselves as spiritual-political leaders of a renewed Islamic world: "To attain the leadership of mankind, we must have something to offer besides material progress, and this other quality can only be a faith and a way of life that both promotes the benefits of modern science and technology and fulfils basic human needs."[26] Given the pervasive evil that he saw abroad in the modern world, Qutb explicitly ruled out negotiation or compromise: "We will not change our own values and concepts . . . to make a bargain with this jahili society. Never!"[27] Instead, he reinterpreted the Islamic tradition of jihad (religious striving and struggle) in such a way that spiritual struggle against the believer's own irreligious and immoral impulses—to which the prophet Muhammad had referred as "the greater jihad"—was deemphasized, subsumed by the "lesser jihad" of holy war against unbelievers and their treacherous allies in the Muslim world. Insofar as the Muslim world was perceived to be under attack by the forces of evil, traditionally binding obligations of "defensive jihad" could be invoked. "For Qutb," Esposito tells us, "jihad, as armed struggle in defense of Islam against the injustice and oppression of anti-Islamic governments and the neocolonialism of the West and the East (Soviet Union) was incumbent upon all Muslims."[28]

At about the same time that the Islamist resurgence inspired by Qutb and others was beginning to gather steam, OPEC began to assert collective control over the supply, and thus the price, of oil in world markets. Oil exporting countries had long felt resentment at the power that multinational oil companies held over the production and marketing of oil which, after all, was pumped from within their own sovereign territory. They wanted to assert greater control over their resources and their national destinies. Further, since world market prices for oil were conventionally denominated in U.S. dollars, oil producing countries earned revenues in dollars and so were hurt by devaluations of the U.S. dollar following President Nixon's 1971 dissolution of the gold–dollar relationship (recall from our discussion in chapter 2 the significance of the gold–dollar linkage within the Bretton Woods system). Since dollars were now worth less on world markets, the oil they sold for dollars was also worth less, as were the very substantial deposits still in the ground. This situation created a substantial incentive to try to raise, and maintain, the world market price of oil. The 1973 Yom Kippur War between Egypt and Syria on one side, and Israel on the other, provided the occasion and the necessary political unity among Arab members of OPEC. Prompted in part by American support for Israel, they agreed to reduce oil production and embargo shipments to the U.S. As world oil supplies tightened in the face of increasing demand, the world market price of oil quadrupled in short order. Petroleum prices shot up even further during the second oil crisis that attended the Iranian Revolution of 1979. This ratcheting upward of oil prices resulted in a massive infusion of petrodollars into the major oil-producing countries, especially Saudi Arabia.[29] In an effort to maintain its legitimacy in the eyes of conservative Muslim subjects, the extravagantly corrupt and autocratic Saudi royal family used this windfall to subsidize fundamentalist Sunni Islamic institutions, media, conferences, and movements worldwide, spreading the writings and speeches of leading Islamist scholars and activists and thereby "creating an international Islamist discourse."[30] It was in the context of this well-funded transnational Islamic revivalist discourse that Qutb's calls for defensive jihad could resonate so strongly.

During the 1980s the U.S. government, Saudi Arabia, and Pakistan (each for their own reasons) poured vast amounts of money and military aid into the jihad then being waged against Soviet invaders by Islamic fighters in Afghanistan. This was the birthplace of al-Qaeda and the training ground for thousands of fighters from around the Islamic world who would later form a recruiting pool for transnational terrorist networks seeking to attack the U.S. and its allies.[31] And it was in the Afghan war that Saudi millionaire Osama bin Laden reconstructed himself as a leading sponsor and symbol of jihad. During his studies at King Abdul Aziz University in Saudi Arabia, bin Laden had been taught by Muhammad Qutb—brother of Sayyid Qutb, the paradigmatic modern Islamist militant and martyr. Also heavily influenced by Qutb was another teacher at the Saudi university attended by bin Laden: Sheikh Abdullah Azzam. Palestinian by birth, Azzam was himself a leading Islamist scholar-militant, a founder of Hamas, and a key recruiter and organizer of the jihadi volunteers from around the Islamic world pouring into Afghanistan in the 1980s to fight the Soviet invaders. Azzam became bin Laden's mentor in the Afghan jihad, working with him to create "the Office of Services, a support organization for Arab volunteers [in the anti-Soviet jihad] that would evolve in the course of time to become the core of al Qaeda."[32] It was after Azzam was killed in 1989 that bin Laden assumed leadership of the organization that would become al Qaeda.

So, in light of all this, it should come as little surprise that Sayyid Qutb's thought echoes in the jihadi declarations of bin Laden and the al Qaeda network. A 1998 fatwa (religious edict) issued by bin Laden and allied Islamists under the name World Islamic Front called for "Jihad against Jews and Crusaders" and listed three major grievances against the U.S. in particular:

- the presence of U.S. military forces within Saudi Arabia, land of Islam's holiest places, "plundering its riches, dictating to its rulers, humiliating its people, terrorizing its neighbors, and turning its bases in the Peninsula into a spearhead through which to fight the neighboring Muslim peoples";
- the use of Saudi bases by the U.S. in its campaign to isolate and strangle Saddam Hussein's Baathist regime in Iraq, and "the great devastation inflicted on the Iraqi people by the crusader-Zionist alliance"

through massive aerial bombardment and a decade of crippling economic sanctions; and

- U.S. support for Israel and "its occupation of Jerusalem and murder
of Muslims [in Palestine]."[33]

On the basis of this not entirely implausible interpretation of recent
history, bin Laden and company see an American hand behind the threats
posed to Islam by the modern world of jahiliyya and argue that all Muslims
are obligated to fight against the U.S.: "All these crimes and sins committed
by the Americans are a clear declaration of war on God, his messenger, and
Muslims. And ulema [Islamic religious scholars] have throughout Islamic
history unanimously agreed that the jihad is an individual duty if the
enemy destroys the Muslim countries." Therefore, bin Laden declares,
Muslims are required "to kill the Americans and their allies—civilians and
military . . . in order to liberate the al-Aqsa Mosque and the holy mosque
[Mecca] from their grip, and in order for their armies to move out of all
the lands of Islam, defeated and unable to threaten any Muslim."[34]

The modern story of globalization is in many ways integral to the emergence of Islamist terrorism. Osama bin Laden, al Qaeda, and more-or-less
loosely affiliated networks of Islamist militants worldwide are drawing on
religious, cultural, and political resources of long standing within the Muslim world; but they have used the ideas of jahiliyya and jihad much as Qutb
did, to make sense of a modern world in which the integrity of Islam and
the dignity of Muslims appears to be threatened, and to respond to that
threat by waging holy war against those perceived as the enemies of Islam.
In the contemporary world, the primary threat to Islamic integrity appears
to emanate from the global strategic, economic, and cultural dominance of
the U.S., embodied in the liberal capitalist world order that U.S. policy has
sought to create over the last sixty years. We are not claiming here that bin
Laden is explicitly motivated by hostility to capitalism as such (indeed he
won his credibility as a jihadi leader fighting against the incursion of Soviet
Marxism into the Afghan corner of the Islamic world). Rather, to the extent
that this multidimensional (political, cultural, and economic) U.S.–led
global order—and its driving thirst for the petroleum concentrated beneath areas of the world in which Muslims predominate—directly and indirectly impinges upon and undermines Muslim ways of life, it elicits from
militant Islamists responses framed in the idiom of defensive jihad. Further
linking contemporary jihad with globalization, the networks of Islamist
militants who take it upon themselves to enact this jihad are present in
most of the world thanks in part to modern global transportation systems
and the transnational diasporas they facilitate. From airline routes criss-

crossing the world to global financial networks, from cell phones and satellite links to the Internet, modern jihadists operating through decentralized and dispersed networks are fully adept at using contemporary technologies of transportation and communication associated with the leading edge of globalization to maintain a sense of collective identity and common purpose and to coordinate their actions. It was this Islamist globalization-within-globalization that brought the horrors of September 11 to the U.S., perpetrated the Madrid train-bombings, the Bali night-club bombing, and a series of other attacks worldwide; and will in all likelihood continue similar attacks against those perceived as aggressing against the Islamic world.

From a Gramscian viewpoint, however, the militance of hard-core Islamists and the violent rage of the terrorists is only the most painfully obvious manifestation of a deeper set of issues involving U.S. relations with the larger Muslim world. As public opinion about the U.S. has soured worldwide, large majorities of people across the Arab world told pollster Zogby International that "U.S. policies, rather than American values, shaped their overall attitudes."[35] Again, John Esposito helps to put this in context:

> Anti-Americanism is driven not by the blind hatred of the terrorists but also by broader-based anger and frustration with American foreign policy among many in Arab and Muslim societies: government officials, diplomats, the military, businessmen, professionals, intellectuals, and journalists. [Many] have graduated from and send their children to Western schools. . . . [They] admire many of the [same] principles and values (political participation, accountability, the basic freedoms of speech, thought, and the press). But they also believe that these principles are applied selectively or not at all when it comes to the Muslim world.[36]

In short, the Islamic world is not monolithic, it is not culturally driven to "hate our freedom," and it is not historically destined (by virtue of such ancient conflicts as the Crusades, the conquest and reconquest of Iberia, or Ottoman expansion into southeastern Europe) to seek mortal combat with Western infidels. Militants and terrorists do not necessarily speak for Islam as a whole; there are many different ways of being a Muslim in the modern world. So it is conceivable that Western governments, and America in particular, could build more just, equitable, and cooperative relations with the Islamic world and especially with those currents of "modernist" Islam that "endeavor to reconcile differences between traditional religious doctrine and secular scientific rationalism, between unquestioning faith and reasoned logic, and between the continuity of Islamic tradition and modernity."[37] If successfully pursued, such a course would weaken the ability of militant Islamists to frame their political agendas in terms that resonate with "popular common sense" across the Islamic world, would isolate the militants from a popular base of support within the larger ummah, and would thus minimize their political influence and the magnitude of the dangers they pose. By pursuing an aggressive, neoimperial policy in the Middle East, the U.S. instead politically strengthens Islamist radicals and courts tragedy of world-historical magnitude.[38]

The Bush Doctrine and the Neoimperial Moment

The most hawkish and hard-line elements in the Bush administration (the Cheney-Rumsfeld-Wolfowitz axis) exploited the atmosphere of jingoism and fear in the U.S. following the terrorist attacks of September 11, 2001, to put into effect their long-cherished vision of U.S. global military supremacy, unilateral action, and the preemptive use of military force deployed to create a world in which the American model of capitalist democracy is unquestioned. This strategy has its immediate roots in Dick Cheney's Defense Department during the waning days of the first Bush administration, when defense officials Zalmay Khalilzad and Lewis Libby (under the supervision of Paul Wolfowitz) drafted a document known as the 1992 *Defense Planning Guidance* (DPG), envisioning a post–Cold War world in which America's position of power and privilege would be beyond challenge.[39]

The incoming Clinton administration, with its more multilateral neoliberalism, displaced the ultra-hawks from the executive branch, but they continued to build on the foundation laid out in the DPG strategy. With the leadership of neoconservative publisher William Kristol,[40] in 1997 they formed an association called the Project for a New American Century (PNAC), dedicated to persuading Americans that "we need to accept responsibility for America's unique role in preserving and extending an international order friendly to our security, our prosperity, and our principles"—all of which PNAC understood to require "a Reaganite policy of military strength and moral clarity" projected on a global scale.[41] Kristol's New Citizenship Project (which served as midwife to PNAC) as well as PNAC itself have been supported by regular infusions of cash from leading conservative foundations such as the Bradley Foundation, the Sarah Scaife Foundation, and the John M. Olin Foundation. These major donors, along with a few others, have for decades strategically invested in the development of right-wing think tanks, quasi-academic institutes, conservative magazines and journals, researchers, polemicists, and policy networks. All of this contributed mightily to the ideological infrastructure of the Reagan revolution and the ratcheting rightward of American political culture over the last twenty-five or thirty years. It was this hothouse environment of conservative funding and ideas that, during the 1990s, sustained and nurtured the ultra-hawks and gave birth to their foreign policy vehicle, PNAC.[42]

PNAC formulated a comprehensive statement of U.S. defense policy that built on the DPG premise that global order "must have a secure foundation on unquestioned U.S. military preeminence."[43] PNAC principals have been clear and explicit that the American-centered world order they seek to strengthen is not just a matter of superordinate power, but is also a superior moral order: "The American-led world that emerged after the Cold War is a more just world than any imaginable alternative." What PNAC advocates, then, is "preserving and reinforcing America's benevolent global hegemony," a policy based on "the blending of principle with material interest" which takes "its meaning and coherence from being rooted in universal principles first enunciated in the *Declaration of Independence*."[44] In this view, the principled exercise of extraordinary American power entails confronting potentially threatening authoritarian states with the aim of transforming them into putatively more pacific liberal democracies, as PNAC executive director Gary Schmidt explained: "The hard truth is that unless you change some of these regimes, you're going to be hard-pressed to get rid of the threat. Liberal democracies don't go to war with one another."[45] As early as January 1998, PNAC's heavy-hitters were collectively and publicly calling on the Clinton administration to use military force for regime change in Iraq.[46]

Among the PNAC principals recruited into the Bush II administration were Cheney as vice president and Libby as his chief of staff, Rumsfeld and Wolfowitz at defense, Richard Perle at the advisory Defense Policy Board, John Bolton in the State Department, and Zalmay Khalilzad and Elliott Abrams at the National Security Council. Even the Bush administration's trade representative, Robert Zoellick—whose portfolio includes management of U.S. relations with arguably the most powerful multilateral global governance institution, the WTO—signed on to the PNAC global agenda.[47] It is not altogether surprising, then, that the Bush administration's strategic response to 9/11 bears a clear resemblance to the policies advocated by PNAC and envisioned in the 1992 DPG.

Made public in September, 2002, Bush's *National Security Strategy for the United States* clearly and explicitly outlines a long-term vision of U.S. global predominance based on military power, a world in which the U.S. would face no serious military competitors and tolerate no challenges to its interests and its authority, and in which the U.S. government would feel free to use preemptive military strikes against those perceived to be potential emergent challengers or who deviate from the administration's putatively universal model of "freedom, democracy, and free enterprise." Exploiting "a position of unparalleled military strength and great economic and political influence"—a unipolar condition to which Bush refers as "a balance of power that favors freedom"—"The United States will use this moment of opportunity to extend the benefits of freedom across the globe. We will actively work to bring the hope of democracy, development, free markets, and free trade to every corner of the globe."[48]

The new U.S. *National Security Strategy* represents a dangerous synthesis of commitments to unilateralism, military supremacy, and the preemptive use of force, all justified by a messianic presumption of American moral superiority: "America will act against . . . emerging threats before they are fully formed":

> Through our willingness to use force in our own defense and in defense of others, the United States demonstrates its resolve to maintain a balance of power that favors freedom. . . . The United States must and will maintain the capability to defeat any attempt by an enemy . . . to impose its will on the United States, our allies, or our friends. . . . Our forces will be strong enough to dissuade potential adversaries from pursuing a military build-up in hopes of surpassing, or equaling, the power of the United States.[49]

And indeed the Bush administration called for substantial increases in U.S. military spending to support this new strategy. Already in a league by itself, the U.S. military budget for 2004 grew to very nearly $400 billion, over six times as great as the next biggest military spender.[50] But even this is not enough for the ultra-hawks: PNAC characterized it as a "modest" increase, resulting in a defense budget that was "inadequate" insofar as "American strength is the key to building the new world you [Bush] have envisioned."[51]

Soon after releasing the new *National Security Strategy*, Mr. Bush gave a highly publicized speech in which he misrepresented controversial suppositions as facts and used the most lurid language to paint Saddam Hussein's Iraq—with its (alleged) stockpiles of chemical and biological weapons, its (supposed) nuclear weapons programs, and its (imputed) ties to al Qaeda and other terrorist groups—as precisely the kind of danger his preemptive strategy was designed for: "Knowing these realities," declared the president, "America must not ignore the threat gathering against us. Facing clear evidence of peril, we cannot wait for final proof—the smoking gun—which could come in the form of a mushroom cloud."[52] While the Bush administration and its supporters were steering the U.S. toward a course of overt militarism, global public opinion was overwhelmingly against an American attack on Iraq.[53] The global justice movement and a broad array of other groups mobilized quickly against the impending war. Coordinated antiwar protests involving perhaps as many as eleven million persons occurred more or less simultaneously on February 15, 2003, in several hundred cities worldwide. In the face of a global peace movement of unprecedented scope and dissension among traditional allies reluctant to follow Uncle Sam to war in Iraq, the Bush administration reiterated fabulous claims about Iraqi weapons of mass destruction and alleged ties to al Qaeda. These claims were problematic even when they were first made and proved insufficient to convince a mostly skeptical world but were remarkably successful in eliciting the consent of American citizens for Bush's bellicose policies.

Recall from chapter 1 that our Gramscian approach to understanding politics emphasizes the means of consent, as well as coercion; therefore the Bush administration's ability to mobilize broad segments of the American public behind its thinly justified war represents a significant political puzzle for us. An important part of the explanation, we believe, lies in the power of a particular kind of patriotism deeply embedded in U.S. popular culture; the rise of popular and militantly conservative media; and the ability of administration hard-liners and their allies to use these cultural resources to rally supporters, marginalize dissenters, and set the dominant tone for public discourse about the war. In addition to newspapers, magazines, and journals in which neoconservative commentators were ensconced, strongly conservative broadcast media such as the Fox TV network (owned by global media mogul Rupert Murdoch), Clear Channel radio network (which has over 1,200 stations and claims 110 million listeners), and a plethora of right-wing talk radio programs lent more-or-less continuous support to the Bush administration's pretexts for war.[54] President Bush had said repeatedly that there could be only two sides in "the war on terror": "You're either with us or against us." Following his cue, conservative media often suggested that anyone who criticized—or even questioned—administration policies was, in effect, supporting terrorists.

Survey evidence indicates that conservative media—and the larger atmosphere of unquestioning jingoism they helped to excite—had a powerful effect on public support for the war: "In the run-up to the war with Iraq and in the postwar period, a significant portion of the American public has held a number of misperceptions that have played a key role in generating and maintaining approval for the decision to go to war." These "misperceptions"—actively fostered by the Bush administration—included the belief that Iraq was involved in the 9/11 attacks, that Iraq actually possessed weapons of mass destruction, and that world public opinion favored a U.S.-led war. "A majority of 60 percent [of the U.S. public] had at least one of these three unambiguous misperceptions." But some media watchers were more likely to be misled than others. In particular, persons who got the bulk of their news from Fox "were most likely to hold misperceptions—and were more than twice as likely than the next nearest network to hold all three misperceptions." The anchorage of these "misperceptions" in popular common sense was profoundly consequential: "Before and after the war, those who have held misperceptions have been far more supportive of the decision to go to war with Iraq" and belief in more than one of them translated into "sharply higher support for the war."[55]

Veteran foreign correspondent Christiane Amanpour explained how the atmosphere of misinformed hyperpatriotism created by the administration and its allies in the conservative media led to self-censorship in more mainstream news outlets like CNN: "I think the press was muzzled, and I think the press self-muzzled. I'm sorry to say, but certainly television and, perhaps, to a certain extent, my station was intimidated by the administration and its foot soldiers at Fox News. And it did, in fact, put a climate of fear and self-censorship, in my view, in terms of the kind of broadcast work we did." When asked about Amanpour's indictment of the media, a Fox News spokesperson responded by suggesting (all too predictably) that Amanpour was on the wrong side in the war on terror: "Given the choice, it's better to be viewed as a foot soldier for Bush than a spokeswoman for al-Qaeda."[56] In an important review of prewar journalism, Michael Massing described the climate in which U.S. journalists worked and implied that Amanpour's analysis was broadly accurate:

> With a popular president promoting war, Democrats in Congress were reluctant to criticize him. . . . Many readers, meanwhile, were intolerant of articles critical of the President. Whenever the Washington Post ran such pieces, reporter Dana Priest recalls, "We got tons of hate mail and threats, calling our patriotism into question." Fox News, Rush Limbaugh, and the Weekly Standard, among others, all stood ready to pounce on journalists who strayed, branding them liberals or traitors—labels that could permanently damage a career. Gradually, journalists began to muzzle themselves.[57]

Well after the fact, prestigious mainstream news outlets such as the *New York Times* and the *Washington Post* publicly, and somewhat lamely, admitted that they had been too credulous about administration claims about Iraq and had not taken seriously enough questions raised by critics of the administration's rush to war.[58]

Having done its best to create the public (mis)impression that attacking Iraq was essential to the war on terror, the Bush administration launched its blitzkrieg on March 19, 2003. While the administration's stated reasons for the attack were specious, the rush to war in Iraq may be understood as an expression of the doctrine of global military dominance. From the perspective of a strategy that sought, in essence, to intimidate the world through the prospect of overwhelming U.S. force, it would have seemed intolerable to watch Saddam Hussein not only surviving the first Gulf war and the subsequent decade of economic sanctions and subversion but continuing to thumb his nose at the United States. Saddam's survival and defiance of U.S. power in a region of such enormous strategic significance effectively mocked the Bush administration's pretensions to unquestioned global supremacy. That removing Saddam was a high priority for those who formulated the Bush doctrine should not then be surprising. The administration also hoped that a postwar client regime in Iraq would provide the U.S. with a base of operations in the heart of the Gulf region more reliably open to U.S. forces than Saudi bases. Further, among the more deluded of the neocons, it was believed that a forcefully "democratized" Iraq would lead to the spread of liberal democracy throughout the Middle East and lessen the perceived threats posed to Israel.[59]

Not entirely irrelevant to these strategic calculations was the fact that Iraq sits atop oil reserves estimated as second only to those of Saudi Arabia, so U.S. dominance in postwar Iraq would provide a reliable source of supply as well as significant leverage over OPEC and global oil markets. Petroleum is America's single most important energy source, representing about two-fifths of total U.S. energy consumption, its primary transportation fuel (in post-Fordist America, transportation accounts for more than two-thirds of total U.S. oil consumption), and a critical power source for its global military machine. With domestic production steadily dwindling and demand growing, at the start of the twenty-first century the U.S. found itself dependent on imports to supply the majority of its petroleum needs. Currently, the sources of U.S. oil imports are more diverse than is commonly imagined, with about a quarter of total U.S. crude oil imports coming from the Persian Gulf region. Although Saudi Arabia is America's single biggest supplier of crude oil, Canada and Mexico are also major suppliers.[60] But U.S. dependence on imported oil continues to grow—as does the petroleum consumption of Europe, Japan, and rapidly industrializing countries like India and China—and no other petroleum reserves are as vast, or as significant for the future of global strategic power, as those of the Gulf region. The Bush administration's National Energy Policy Task Force, chaired by Vice President Cheney, estimated that the Gulf region will be supplying around two-thirds of the world's oil needs by the year 2020. In their quest for global supremacy, Bush administration officials may well have believed that militarily-based strategic dominance in the Middle East, and an American hand on the world's oil tap, would represent a bargaining chip of incalculable value when dealing with potentially incompliant allies (Europe, Japan) and emergent rivals (especially China) even more dependent on imported oil than the U.S. itself.[61]

Clearly, then, we don't discount U.S. interests in Persian Gulf oil in attempting to make sense of the drive for war in Iraq. However, we are skeptical of crudely mechanical explanations of the sort in which particular capitalists or corporations are seen to be the puppet-masters pulling the strings of government. This sort of reasoning underlies popular versions of the "blood for oil" story, which posits that (a) U.S. oil companies wanted possession of Iraqi oil, (b) Bush and Cheney were oil men, and (c) therefore the war was fundamentally about securing direct possession of Iraqi oil for U.S.-based oil companies. In contrast to such simpleminded "blood for oil" narratives, we would argue for a more nuanced version of the relationship among capitalism, oil, and war based on the following two important theoretical claims. First, the state is positioned within capitalist social formations in such a way that, while it is structurally dependent on the investment activities of the capitalist class as a whole and hence bound to seek the reproduction of capitalism, the state is not reducible to a simple instrument of particular elements of that class.[62] While capitalists are not without power and influence, the state is not simply a tool under their direct control, as such "ruling class instrumentalist" explanations presume. Rather, the state constructs a vision of the "national interest" to frame its policies and recruit the support of various social groups and segments of the public. This "national interest" will generally favor overall conditions of business confidence and successful capital accumulation but need not reflect the wishes of particular capitalists. Relatedly, our second theoretical claim is that material interests cannot directly determine the actions of social agents. Such interests become socially meaningful (such that actions premised upon these interests can appear to "make sense") only when interests are seen in the context of a particular worldview or ideology that enables us to make sense of the world and understand our position within it. As emphasized by Antonio Gramsci, it is in and through ideology that people become conscious of, and actors in, fundamental social conflicts.[63] In this view, U.S. interests in Middle East oil do not directly determine state policy but are rather interpreted through the ideological lenses of the national security strategy, which suggests that U.S. strategic dominance of this oil-rich region is crucial to the reproduction of both global strategic dominance and the form of energy-intensive, post-Fordist capitalism within which that dominance is embedded. In PNAC's moral universe, both of these conditions are identified with "freedom" and hence are unambiguously in the general interest of humankind. Any direct benefits that may accrue to particular U.S. oil companies are then icing on the cake. Further weakening a straightforward ruling class instrumentalist account of the war, the global capitalist bloc was sharply divided over U.S. unilateralism and jittery about the economic risks of war. Even oil company executives expressed unease.[64]

The Bush administration has not, of course, abandoned the long-standing U.S. commitment to the deepening of neoliberal capitalist relations on a global basis. Indeed, the Bush doctrine explicitly elevates free trade to the status of "a moral principle," handed down to us along with liberty and democracy as part of the heritage of Western civilization, presumed to be universally valid and generally applicable as aspects of "a single sustainable model for national success: freedom, democracy, and free enterprise":

> The lessons of history are clear: market economies, not command-and-control economies with the heavy hand of government, are the best way to promote prosperity and reduce poverty. Policies that further strengthen market incentives and market institutions are relevant for all economies.[65]

The institutional forms associated with neoliberal capitalism are explicitly integrated into U.S. national security strategy: "pro-growth legal and regulatory policies to encourage business investment"; "lower marginal tax rates"; conservative fiscal policies (no small irony here, as the U.S. racks up unprecedented federal budget deficits); free trade and international capital flows.[66] Whereas for much of the preceding decade, the core rationale of neoliberalism had been to use (primarily if not exclusively) multilateral and cooperative means to separate politics from economics to the greatest extent possible and thus to mystify the workings of power within the global capitalist economy, the new national security strategy directly and explicitly links neoliberal capitalism with American global military dominance. The institutional concomitant of this shift in the balance of coercion and consent—as well as the underlying continuity of the U.S.-led global capitalist project—is well summarized by Leo Panitch and Sam Gindin:

> Perhaps the most important change in the administrative structure of the American empire in the transition from the Clinton administration to the Bush II administration has been the displacement of the Treasury [Department] from its pinnacle at the top of the state apparatus. The branches of the American state that control and dispense the means of violence are now in the driver's seat; in an administration representing a Republican Party

that has always been made up of a coalition of free marketers, social conservatives and military hawks, the balance has been titled decisively by September 11th toward the latter. But the unconcealed imperial face that the American state is now prepared to show the world above all pertains to the increasing difficulties of managing a truly global informal empire—a problem that goes well beyond any change from administration to administration.[67]

The Bush strategy thus entails both continuities and discontinuities in relation to previous U.S. policy. Attempting to secure the political conditions of U.S.-centered global capitalism in a world of multiple sovereign states, the new strategy shifts the global balance of coercion and consent significantly toward the more coercive side of power. It is in this sense that the present conjuncture represents a "neoimperial moment" within the historical development of U.S.-led global capitalism. As we are already seeing, this reemphasis on coercive power may have the effect of rendering the power relations of neoliberal world order (or some of them at any rate) more visible and more difficult effectively to legitimate on a global basis. Popular resentment of American neoimperial policies worldwide, especially among erstwhile allies, remains strong. In Islamic countries, Osama bin Laden is viewed as a symbol of resistance to U.S. power, and it is that which accounts for his continuing popularity.[68] It is difficult to see how such a manifestly coercive—and almost universally reviled—form of world order is politically sustainable.

While a change in the White House might lessen the hard edge of U.S. neoimperialism, it is not at all clear that a Democratic administration would enact a postimperial global policy. Interviews with Kerry campaign foreign policy advisors and analysis of the foreign policy planks of the Democratic Party platform strongly suggest that a Democratic administration would seek more multilateral means for managing the political challenges of globalization, reemphasizing diplomacy and employing "a careful synthesis of armed power, peacekeeping capacity, international institutions, and non-governmental organizations," but would retain the trump card of U.S. global military supremacy and leave the door open for unilateral and preemptive uses of force: "[W]e will never wait for a green light from abroad when our safety is at stake."[69] While these are not trivial differences—especially in the climate of pervasive global anti-Americanism that the neoimperial turn has incited—they are differences over means rather than fundamental ends. A common denominator of U.S. politics is the vision of American exceptionalism and the warrant this provides for maintaining a world order built around U.S. values, interests, and power.

Conclusion

Contemporary capitalist globalization and U.S. power are intimately entwined. For most of its history, the U.S. has sought to promote international trade and investment by U.S.-based firms and has on numerous occasions used imperial exercises of military force to maintain abroad a climate friendly to U.S.-based capital. For more than fifty years, the U.S. has pursued systematically a global order supportive of capitalism as an integral part of U.S. national security. This U.S.-centered global order cannot be adequately understood solely in terms of interstate politics or market transactions; it is rather a multidimensional system in which political, economic, and cultural aspects were deeply intertwined. While U.S. power has been central to the construction of this increasingly unequal world, and coercive force has never been entirely absent, the relative balance between coercive and consensual forms of power has varied.

Increasingly important to this petroleum-powered global capitalist system have been the incomparable oil reserves of the Persian Gulf region. Since World War II, the U.S. has used both diplomacy and imperial force to maintain political dominance in the Gulf. As the twentieth century waned, there arose among the predominantly Muslim peoples of the Middle East a militant minority willing to use violence to resist the political, cultural, and economic incursions of this U.S.-led global system. Reinterpreting Islamic traditions in ways that authorize terrorist attacks on the U.S., its citizens, and its allies—as well as Muslims deemed heretical, insufficiently pious, or politically inconvenient—these Islamist militants have shown themselves to be highly adept at exploiting the transnational networks and technologies of communication and transportation fostered by capitalist globalization. In light of their ideological power, technological sophistication, and transnational presence, Islamist militants may be perceived as posing a significant threat not just to homeland security, but potentially to U.S. power in the Gulf and the surrounding region, and therefore to the U.S.-centered global order, which depends on the maintenance of that power. It is in this context that the self-righteous ideology of the "war on terror" has been deployed to authorize neoimperial military interventions in the Gulf, the Middle East, and Central Asia, and indeed across much of the Islamic world. This projection of U.S. military power into the Islamic world has strengthened, rather than weakened, the political bases of support for the most militant of the Islamist tendencies.

With these developments, some of the power relations underlying contemporary globalization have burst into the open as explicit terrains of struggle. Globalizing capitalism and neoimperial adventures are two sides of a system of global power now facing increasing resistance along multiple dimensions, from myriad civil society groups seeking to democratize the global economy and create a more equitable world, to a global peace movement trying to rein in imperial aggression, to Islamist radicals seeking to expel U.S. power from the Islamic world to reconstruct what they consider to be a divinely sanctioned moral-political order. We cannot see far into the future to predict how these struggles will eventuate, but we can say with confidence that globalization can no longer be credibly represented as an inevitable, apolitical, and universally beneficial process of market-based integration. Nor can its politics adequately be described in terms of traditional categories of interstate competition and rivalry. Our world is much more complex and open-ended than mainstream theories of IPE are able to comprehend, and our case for critical theory of global politics rests on its ability to illuminate these tensions and possibilities.

CONCLUSION

Globalization and International Political Economy: So What?

As we argue throughout this book, globalization means that our world is changing and we are changing along with it. Our economic, political, and cultural relations, even our intimate lives, are being transformed. From what we do at work, to the products we buy and the "lifestyles" we live, to the power relations that subordinate and privilege us on scales from the household to the global, all are bound up together in complex processes of change. One of the central messages of this book, however, is that these processes are not predetermined or ineluctable. Globalization is not just something that happens to us; it is also, and just as important, *something we are doing collectively.* When we view it this way, we see that implicit within processes of capitalist globalization are possibilities for a variety of future possible worlds. As we argue in chapter 1, the task of critical theory is to illuminate some of those possibilities, the social relations that give rise to them, and the political struggles that may lead toward realization of some alternative possible worlds rather than others. That is what is at stake in debates over globalization and international political economy. What may at first appear as an arcane squabble among scholars is in fact part of a conversation about the kind of world we will live in and the ways in which we will live in it—the kind of persons we will become in this globalizing world. Since it will profoundly affect your lives, it is a conversation in which you should be ready to participate. Our hope is that what you have read in this book will help prepare you for that conversation.

We argue in chapter 2 that capitalism, modernity, and globalization have been historically intertwined in such intimate ways that it is misleading to represent these processes in terms of the voluntary, spontaneous, and mutually beneficial spread of market relations among essentially autonomous and self-interested individuals—as is suggested by the Smithian views that predominate in mainstream economics. Instead, we claim, the apparent triumph of globalizing capitalism is, at its core, a *political* story in which the appearance of naturalness and inevitability masks the ways in which global power relations are being actively reconstructed and contested. Insofar as capitalism has been interwoven with modern political states as well as power relations based on gender and race, critical analysis of the class powers of capitalism appears to us as integral to critical analysis of the modern social world. Accordingly, we sketched the history of capitalist class relations as they emerged from the dispossession of peasant farmers in eighteenth-century England and the creation of a landless, market-dependent working class with nothing to sell but their labor, through the first industrial revolution and the subsequent rise of the nineteenth-century free trade system sponsored by Britain, and the twentieth-century emergence of Fordist production systems in the U.S., which paved the way for the post–World War II capitalist world order. We traced the late-twentieth-century transition from Fordist globalization aspiring toward a rough correspondence of mass production and mass consumption to the more flexible, but also relentlessly competition-driven and austere, form of global capitalism known as neoliberalism. At various stages in our historical overview, we have tried to suggest some of the ways in which capitalist class relations have been bound up with race and gender-based forms of social power and domination. The politics of globalization is much more complex than a simple story of class relations—derived from an old-fashioned, more fundamentalist Marxism—is able to comprehend. While we want to affirm that critical analysis of class and class-based power is necessary to understanding capitalist globalization, we do not want to be misunderstood as suggesting that this is by itself sufficient.

In this book we argue that contemporary globalization—driven by the capitalist imperative of boundless competitive accumulation, and generating unprecedented time–space compression—is qualitatively distinct from other forms of extensive social interaction that may have preceded it. As shown in chapter 2, contemporary capitalism has created the infrastructure of globalized production and finance, which together imply that the entire process of capital accumulation—from investment, to production, to sale of the product and reinvestment of surplus—is no longer anchored within the territorial bounds of particular nation-states. We highlight (in chapter 4) the globalization of labor and new patterns of migration that are directly linked to emerging transnational labor markets and the incipient deterritorialization of the state. As countries like the Philippines have sought to enhance their foreign exchange earnings and reduce their international debt by exporting gendered labor, flows of migrant domestic workers have spread to numerous countries, stretching the boundaries of political community and suggesting the potential emergence of new forms of deterritorialized citizenship and transnational labor organization. We further emphasize the ways in which processes of globalization have engendered new forms of political activity, the globalization of ideological struggle, as emergent transnational networks struggle over the meanings of globalization and the implications for future possible worlds. We seek to exemplify these emergent forms of global politics in chapter 3 by tracing the emergence of the World Economic Forum as a vehicle for formulating among global capitalists and their allies a potentially hegemonic vision of capitalist globalization, under the supposedly benign management of global capitalists. This vision is encapsulated in the WEF's motto "entrepreneurship in the public interest." We show how the WEF manifests the contradictory character of capitalist class power—simultaneously *private* and *social*—by representing itself to the world as a kind of global public sphere while at the same time maintaining its character as an exclusive club by restricting its membership to corporate capitalists willing and able to pay large fees to the Forum. But the development of this global hegemonic project has not gone unopposed. We also note the emergence of alternative visions of "globalization from below" enacted by new kinds of transnational political actors such as the Zapatista movement and associated global support networks, the Global Justice Movement, which coalesced in order to oppose the neoliberal form of capitalist globalization, and the global antiwar movement seeking to restrain U.S. militarism and imperial domination.

None of this, we stress, should be construed as suggesting that nation-states no longer matter, for as shown in chapter 5, interstate politics remains an essential part of these global webs of economic, cultural, and political relations. While we point to the rise of global civil society as a significant aspect of the politics of globalization, we believe just as strongly that it is a mistake to declare a borderless world in which increasingly irrelevant nation-states are destined to fade away. Nation-states and ideologies of nationalism are still with us, still shaping how we see ourselves and how we relate to one another in a globalizing world. Despite the efforts of global civil society activists to construct a culture of transnational solidarity, mutual respect, and reciprocal responsibility, Americans appear to understand themselves as privileged actors in the world, a special kind of global leader whose dominant power is seen to be the reflection of , and to be authorized by, its presumed moral and civilizational superiority. As the world's most powerful nation-state conducts its policy according to official double standards and self-righteously imposes its will on most of the rest of the world, the rise of intense and widespread anti-Americanism should not be surprising. In the context of a post–Cold War world in which American power is unrivaled but far from omnipotent; in which American-led globalization has produced rapid cultural change and historic levels of inequality; in which institutions and processes of global governance have emerged but are of questionable legitimacy, limited in capability and subject to disproportionate U.S. power; and in which many (but surely not all) Americans and non-Americans understand in almost diametrically opposed terms the world they must live in together, the stage is set for mutual incomprehension and conflict, terror and counterterror.

There are, then, good reasons to expect that the continuing drama of globalization may entail substantial elements of tragedy; along with new opportunities for many individuals and unprecedented technological marvels may well come growing inequality within and between nations, financial instability and recurrent economic crises, mass poverty and pandemic disease, arrogant power and stubborn resistance, terror and war. Like the capitalist modernity from which it arises, the politics of globalization is profoundly contradictory.

But, as the intellectual tradition of historical materialism reminds us, contradictions entail possibilities. From within the tensions and conflicts inherent in processes of globalization, a variety of social movements and organizations—some explicitly class-identified but many others not—have begun to create a transnational common sense and corresponding forms of political organization and activity. Integral to this project has been the construction of a culture of solidarity, mutual respect, and reciprocity, which transcended national boundaries and formal citizenship. From the poetic visions of Subcomandante Marcos, which animated international Zapatista support networks in the 1990s, to the massive and diverse global justice and peace movements, to migrant domestic workers struggling to organize their collective strength, the rise of progressive transnational political movements offers hope that together human beings may yet make their world anew—more egalitarian, pluralistic, and humane, and ultimately less violent and full of suffering. These visions and the political projects they animate have not disappeared and continue to hold out hope for future possible worlds. If such possibilities are to be realized, it will be essential for students of global political economy to maintain the critical intellectual resources needed to see beyond reified appearances of globalization, to question those appearances, and to recognize that latent within them lie "the possibility and necessity of speaking and listening" in "a world made of many worlds."[1]

NOTES

Chapter 1: The Difference Globalization Makes

1. Mark Rupert, *Ideologies of Globalization* (London: Routledge, 2000).

2. Manfred Steger, *Globalism: The New Market Ideology* (Lanham, MD: Rowman & Littlefield, 2002), chapter 4.

3. For a prominent example of this sort of calumny directed at protesters, see Thomas Friedman, "Senseless in Seattle," *New York Times,* December 1, 1999.

4. Robert Reich, *The Work of Nations* (New York: Addison-Wesley, 1991); Laura Tyson, *Who's Bashing Whom?* (Washington, DC: Institute for International Economics, 1992).

5. The issues surrounding dialectical theory are complex and philosophically deep, and we do not attempt to elucidate them here. Suffice it to say for our purposes that dialectical ways of thinking are wary of oversimplified, static dichotomies of either/or, instead looking for historically shifting interrelations between entities that might, on first glance, appear as simple opposites. Among the more important of these are fact and value, theory and practice, freedom and unfreedom, labor and capital. In a dialectical view, the uneasy relations among such apparently contradictory aspects of modern life give rise to fundamental tensions and possibilities for alternative future worlds. Useful introductions to Marxian dialectical theory include (in ascending order of sophistication and difficulty): Robert Heil-

broner, *Marxism: For and Against* (New York: Norton, 1980); Richard Schmitt, *Introduction to Marx and Engels*, 2d ed. (Boulder: Westview, 1997); Bertell Ollman, *Dance of the Dialectic* (Urbana: University of Illinois Press, 2003).

6. David Harvey, *The Condition of Postmodernity* (Oxford: Blackwell, 1989), 240.

7. John Maynard Keynes, *Economic Consequences of the Peace,* 1919, chapter 2, McMaster University Department of Economics, at socserv2.socsci.mcmaster.ca/~econ/ugcm/3ll3/keynes/peace.htm (accessed September 6, 2004).

8. Karl Marx and Friedrich Engels, "The Communist Manifesto," in *Karl Marx: Selected Writings*, 2d ed., ed. David McLellan, 249 (Oxford: Oxford University Press, 2000).

9. Adam Smith, *Wealth of Nations* (Oxford: Oxford University Press, 1993); Douglas Irwin, *Free Trade under Fire* (Princeton, NJ: Princeton University Press, 2002).

10. For a detailed examination of how American political science has been shaped by, and served to support, U.S. foreign policy goals, see Ido Oren, *Our Enemies and US* (Ithaca, NY: Cornell University Press, 2003).

11. Consistent with dialectical traditions of historical materialism (and various contemporary philosophies of knowledge), we reject the rigid dichotomization of fact and value, theory and practice, and therefore expect the theoretical and research trajectories of social scientists, policy makers, and others within the academic division of labor to be *influenced* by their social position conceived as classed, gendered, geographically and temporally situated, etc. This is quite different, of course, from an argument that knowledge is wholly *determined* by social position.

12. Marx, "The German Ideology," in *Karl Marx: Selected Writings*, 2d ed., ed. David McLellan, 181 (Oxford: Oxford University Press, 2000).

13. Marx, "The German Ideology," 185.

14. Karl Marx, *Capital* (New York: Vintage, 1977), vol. 1, 163–77.

15. Derek Sayer, *Capitalism and Modernity* (London: Routledge, 1991), 88.

16. Karl Marx , "Economic and Philosophical Manuscripts," in *Karl Marx: Early Writings,* 377–78 (London: Penguin, 1975), emphasis in original.

17. Some will object to this line of argument by suggesting that in the most advanced capitalist societies such as the U.S., well-developed stock markets have facilitated widespread ownership of corporate assets. For example, *New York Times* power-pundit Thomas Friedman has celebrated the emergence of an economy in which we are all capitalists: "For the first time in American history both Joe Six-pack and Billionaire Bob are watching CNBC to see how their shares in the market are faring" (*The Lexus and the Olive Tree* [New York: Farrar, Straus & Giroux, 2000], 105). It is crucial to note that even if over half the U.S. population now owns *some* corporate equity (generally stock held by pension plans or mutual funds), ownership of wealth in the form of corporate equities, financial instruments such as bonds, and business assets is densely concentrated in the wealthiest strata of the population. According to Federal Reserve data for 1998, the wealthiest

10 percent of Americans owned over 82 percent of stock and 86 percent of bonds owned by individuals (including indirect ownership through mutual funds) and more than 91 percent of business assets. Ownership of these financial and business assets is even more disproportionately concentrated in the stratospheric regions inhabited by the wealthiest *half of 1 percent* of the population who owned over 31 percent of stocks, almost 32 percent of bonds, and almost 55 percent of business assets: Federal Reserve data reported in Doug Henwood, "Wealth News," *Left Business Observer* 94 (May 5, 2000). It strikes us as remarkable that this situation could be represented as a liquidation of class-based inequalities of wealth and their attendant differentials of social power.

18. Samuel Bowles and Herb Gintis, *Democracy and Capitalism* (New York: Basic, 1986), 90; see also Fred Block, "The Ruling Class Does Not Rule," *Socialist Revolution* 33 (1977): 6–28; and Howard Wachtel, *Money Mandarins* (Armonk, NY: Sharpe), 190–93.

19. Antonio Gramsci, *Selections from the Prison Notebooks* (New York: International Publishers, 1971); see also Mark Rupert, "Globalizing Common Sense: A Marxian-Gramscian (Re-)vision of the Politics of Governance/Resistance," *Review of International Studies* 29 (2003): 181–98.

20. Robert Cox, *Production, Power, and World Order* (New York: Columbia University Press, 1987); and Cox, *Approaches to World Order* (Cambridge: Cambridge University Press, 1996).

21. Smith, *Wealth of Nations*, 21.

22. Ellen Wood, *The Origin of Capitalism* (New York: Monthly Review Press, 1999); and Wood, *Empire of Capital* (London: Verso, 2003).

Chapter 2: A Brief History of Globalization

1. Compare Adam Smith, *Wealth of Nations* (Oxford: Oxford University Press, 1993), 21; Robert Brenner, "The Social Basis of Economic Development," in *Analytical Marxism*, ed. John Roemer, 23–53 (Cambridge: Cambridge University Press, 1986); Ellen Wood, *The Origin of Capitalism* (New York: Monthly Review Press, 1999); and Wood, *Empire of Capital* (London: Verso, 2003).

2. Wood, *Origin*, 69.

3. Wood, *Origin*, 70.

4. Wood, *Origin*, 75.

5. Wood, *Origin*, 78.

6. Wood, *Origin*, 78.

7. Karl Marx, *Capital*, vol. 1, ch. 28: This version is from the 1886 Moore and Aveling translation, available at the Marx and Engels Internet Archive, n.d., www.marxists.org/archive/marx/works/1867-c1/ch28.htm (accessed September 6, 2004).

8. Michelle Barrett, *Women's Oppression Today* (London: Verso, 1988), 219.

9. Wood, *Origin*, 80.

10. Wood, *Origin*, 102.

11. Wood, *Empire of Capital.*

12. For the almost forgotten history of the Belgian Congo, see Adam Hochschild, *King Leopold's Ghost* (Boston: Houghton Mifflin, 1998).

13. Wood, *Empire,* 152, 154.

14. Smith, *Wealth of Nations,* 18.

15. Smith, *Wealth of Nations,* 292–93.

16. See, for example, Robert Cox, *Production, Power, and World Order* (New York: Columbia University Press, 1987), 123–47.

17. Mark Rupert, *Producing Hegemony* (Cambridge: Cambridge University Press, 1995), 67–68.

18. Cox, *Production, Power, and World Order,* 151–64.

19. Quoted in Rupert, *Producing Hegemony,* 111.

20. Rupert, *Producing Hegemony.*

21. Rupert, *Producing Hegemony.*

22. World Trade Organization, *Trading into the Future,* 1st ed. (Geneva: WTO, 1995).

23. World Trade Organization, *Trading into the Future,* 2d ed. (Geneva: WTO, 1998); Lori Wallach and Michelle Sforza, *Whose Trade Organization?* (Washington, DC: Public Citizen/Global Trade Watch, 1999).

24. Robert Brenner, *The Boom and the Bubble: The US in the World Economy* (London: Verso, 2002).

25. Peter Dicken, *Global Shift,* 2d ed. (New York: Guilford, 1992), ch. 2; David Held, A. McGrew, D. Goldblatt, and J. Perraton, *Global Transformations* (Cambridge: Polity, 1999), 171–75.

26. David Harvey, *The Condition of Postmodernity* (Oxford: Blackwell, 1989), chs. 8–9; Rupert, *Producing Hegemony,* ch. 8.

27. Kim Moody, *An Injury to All: The Decline of American Unionism* (London: Verso, 1988); Moody, *Workers in a Lean World* (London: Verso, 1997); David Gordon, *Fat and Mean* (New York: Free Press, 1996).

28. Kate Bronfenbrenner, "We'll Close!" *Multinational Monitor* 18, no. 3 (March 1997), at www.essential.org/monitor/hyper/mm0397.04.html; and Bronfenbrenner, "Raw Power," *Multinational Monitor* 21, no. 12 (December 2000), at www.essential.org/monitor/mm2000/00december/power.html.

29. John Agnew and Stuart Corbridge, *Mastering Space* (London: Routledge, 1995), 169.

30. Agnew and Corbridge, *Mastering Space,* 170.

31. Dicken, *Global Shift,* 47–88; Agnew and Corbridge, *Mastering Space,* 166–71; Held, McGrew, Goldblatt, and Perraton, *Global Transformations,* 171–75, 236–37, 242–82.

32. Held, McGrew, Goldblatt, and Perraton, *Global Transformations,* 246.

33. Dicken, *Global Shift,* 54–56, 64–67, 73–74; Held, McGrew, Goldblatt, and Perraton, *Global Transformations,* 243–45, 248–50, 253–55.

34. Dicken, *Global Shift,* 24–27, 33–40; Held, McGrew, Goldblatt, and Perraton, *Global Transformations,* 171–75.

35. World Bank, *World Development Report 1995* (Oxford: Oxford University Press, 1995), 51.

36. Compare Paul Krugman, "In Praise of Cheap Labor," *Slate* (March 20, 1997), atweb.mit.edu/krugman/www/smokey.html (accessed September 3, 2004); Andrew Ross, *No Sweat* (London: Verso, 1997); and Rachel Kamel and Anya Hoffman, *The Maquiladora Reader* (Philadelphia: American Friends Service Committee, 1999).

37. Howard Wachtel, *The Money Mandarins* (Armonk, NY: Sharpe, 1990), 75.

38. Wachtel, *Money Mandarins*; Agnew and Corbridge, *Mastering Space*, 171–78; Held, McGrew, Goldblatt, and Perraton, *Global Transformations*, 199–235.

39. Wachtel, *Money Mandarins*, 108.

40. Walden Bello, *Dark Victory* (London: Pluto, 1994), 25.

41. Bello, *Dark Victory*, 31.

42. Robin Hahnel, *Panic Rules* (Boston: South End, 1999), 56.

43. Adam Przeworski, quoted in Paul Thomas, *Alien Politics* (London: Routledge, 1994), 153.

44. William Greider, *One World, Ready or Not* (New York: Simon & Schuster, 1997), 298, 308.

45. United Nations, *Human Development Report,* 2002, 19, at hdr.undp.org/reports/global/2002/en/ (accessed September 6, 2004).

46. World Bank, *World Development Report 2000–01*, at econ.worldbank.org/wdr/23 (accessed September 6, 2004).

47. Joseph Stiglitz, *Globalization and Its Discontents* (New York: Norton, 2002), xii, 16, 36, 73–74, 196.

48. Stiglitz, *Globalization*, 55, 74, 76–78, 91–92, 209, 218–19, 247.

49. Stiglitz, *Globalization*, 12–15, 252.

50. Stiglitz, *Globalization*, 18.

51. Stiglitz, *Globalization*, 12, 47.

52. Stiglitz, *Globalization*, 19, 109, 130, 172.

53. Stiglitz, *Globalization*, xiv, 247, 248.

54. Compare WTO, *Trading into the Future*, 2d ed., 51, with Wallach and Sforza, *Whose Trade Organization*, ch. 7; WTO, *Trading into the Future,* 49, with Wallach and Sforza, *Whose Trade Organization,* 15, 22–26; and WTO, *Trading into the Future,* 35, with Wallach and Sforza, *Whose Trade Organization,* 133, 152.

55. Dicken, *Global Shift*, 186; Jan Pettman, *Worlding Women* (London: Routledge, 1996), 168; V. Spike Peterson, *A Critical Rewriting of Global Political Economy* (London: Routledge, 2003), 62–65, 70–76.

56. Cynthia Enloe, *Bananas, Beaches and Bases* (Berkeley: University of California Press, 1989), 162; Pettman, *Worlding Women*, 167–68.

57. Pettman, *Worlding Women,*168–69; Peterson, *Critical Rewriting,* 70–76.

58. Arturo Escobar, *Encountering Development* (Princeton, NJ: Princeton University Press, 1995); Stuart Hall, "The West and the Rest," in *Modernity*, ed. S. Hall, D. Held, D. Hubert, and K. Thompson, 184–227 (Oxford: Blackwell, 1996).

Chapter 3: New Forms of Global Power and Resistance

1. Quotations in the paragraph above are from World Economic Forum, *Committed to Improving the State of the World* (Geneva: WEF, 1997), 10.

2. World Economic Forum, *About the World Economic Forum* (Geneva: WEF, 1997).

3. Charles McLean, "The Case for Davos," *International Herald Tribune,* February 13, 2001. Preceding quotation was McLean quoted in Dan Barry, "Appearing in the Role of Evil: The Other Side," *New York Times,* January 31, 2002.

4. Kees van der Pijl, *Transnational Classes and International Relations* (London: Routledge, 1998), 132–35; for a more skeptical view of the WEF's powers see Jean–Christophe Graz, "How Powerful Are Transnational Elite Clubs? The Social Myth of the World Economic Forum," *New Political Economy* 8, no. 3 (2003): 321–40.

5. Stephanie Strom and Louis Uchitelle, "Economic Forum Moves to Manhattan," *New York Times,* January 27, 2002.

6. Anne Swardson, "Entrance Fees to the Marketplace of Ideas," *Washington Post,* January 24, 2000.

7. Public Citizen/Global Trade Watch, *Davos World Economic Forum: Pricey Corporate Trade Association Loses Its Camouflage* (Washington, DC: Public Citizen, 2002), 14.

8. Public Citizen/Global Trade Watch, *Davos,* 6, 8–9.

9. Klaus Schwab and Claude Smadja, "Start Taking the Backlash Against Globalization Seriously," *International Herald Tribune,* February 1, 1996.

10. World Economic Forum, *Creative Impatience Can Manage Problems of Globalization,* February 1, 1996, at www.weforum.org/frames/press/am96/pr10ph.htm.

11. Klaus Schwab and Claude Smadja, "Globalization Needs a Human Face," *International Herald Tribune,* January 28, 1999.

12. Klaus Schwab, "Finding the Right Balance: Opening Address to Annual Meeting," Davos, 1999, at live99.weforum.org/opening_ksc.asp.

13. Public Citizen/Global Trade Watch, *Davos,* 11.

14. Smadja quoted in Michael Hollingdale, "NGOs Threaten Forum Withdrawal," *Swiss Info,* January 28, 2001, at www.swissinfo.org.

15. Guy de Jonquieres and Holly Yeager, "Davos Goes West," *Financial Times,* January 30, 2002.

16. Public Citizen/Global Trade Watch, *Davos,* 11.

17. I am grateful to Adam Morton for suggesting this syncretic understanding of Zapatista ideology. See also Harry Cleaver, *The Chiapas Uprising and the Future of Class Struggle in the New World Order,* 1994, at www.eco.utexas.edu/facstaff/Cleaver/chiapasuprising.html; Manuel Castells, *The Power of Identity* (Oxford: Blackwell, 1997); John Ross, *The War Against Oblivion* (Monroe, ME: Common Courage Press, 2000); Marcos, *Our Word Is Our Weapon* (New York: Seven Stories Press, 2001).

18. Zapatistas, *Documents from the 1996 Encounter for Humanity and against Neoliberalism* (New York: Seven Stories Press, 1998), 11.

19. Cleaver, *Chiapas Uprising.*

20. Marcos, *Our Word*, 90.

21. Zapatistas, *Documents*, 30.

22. Zapatistas, *Documents*, 43, 47, 45.

23. Marcos, *Our Word*, 18, 33, 44, 49, 72.

24. Zapatistas, *Documents*, 52–54.

25. Michael Hardt and Antonio Negri, *What the Protesters in Genoa Want*, Global Policy Forum, 2001, at www.globalpolicy.org/ngos/role/globdem/globprot/2001/0720rens.htm. Originally published in *New York Times*, July 20, 2001.

26. Dan LaBotz, "Moving for Global Justice," *Against the Current* 88 (September–October 2000), at www.igc.org/solidarity/atc.

27. Naomi Klein, "The Vision Thing," in *The Battle of Seattle*, ed. E. Yuen, G. Katsiaficas, and D. Rose, 312 (New York: Soft Skull Press, 2001); and "Reclaiming the Commons," in *A Movement of Movements*, ed. Tom Mertes (London: Verso, 2004).

28. Maude Barlow and Tony Clarke, *Global Showdown* (Toronto: Stoddart Publishing, 2002), 125, 26, 208.

29. Rudolf Rocker quoted in Noam Chomsky, "Introduction," in *Anarchism*, by D. Guerin, vii, viii (New York: Monthly Review, 1970).

30. Murray Bookchin, *The Murray Bookchin Reader*, ed. Janet Biehl, 131 (London: Cassell, 1997), see also 146–47.

31. Barbara Epstein, "Anarchism and the Anti–Globalization Movement," *Monthly Review* (September 2001), at www.monthlyreview.org/0901epstein.htm.

32. See Epstein, "Anarchism"; William Finnegan, "After Seattle: Anarchists Get Organized," *The New Yorker* (April 17, 2000): 40–51; James Harding, "Counter Capitalism: Inside the Black Bloc," *Financial Times*, October 15, 2001, at specials.ft.com/countercap/FT3BG4GLUSC.html; Esther Kaplan, "Keepers of the Flame," *Village Voice* (January 19, 2002), at www.villagevoice.com/issues/0205/kaplan.php.

33. David Graeber, "Anarchy in the USA," *In These Times*, (January 10, 2000), at www.inthesetimes.com; "The New Anarchists," in *A Movement of Movements*, ed. Tom Mertes, 202–15 (London: Verso, 2004); and "Reinventing Democracy," *In These Times* (February 19, 2002), at www.inthesetimes.com/.

34. David Graeber, "Anarchy," 70; compare Bookchin, *Reader*, 131.

35. Anti-Capitalist Convergence, NY, *Why We Are Not Making Demands of the World Economic Forum*, 2002, at www.accnyc.org/issues_wefdemands.html.

36. David McNally, "Mass Protests in Quebec City: From Anti–Globalization to Anti–Capitalism," *New Politics* 8, no. 3 (2001): 76–86.

37. David Held, A. McGrew, D. Goldblatt, and J. Perraton, *Global Transformations* (Cambridge: Polity, 1999), 53.

38. Andrew Ross, *No Sweat* (London: Verso, 1997); Liza Featherstone, *Students Against Sweatshops* (London: Verso, 2002).

39. Bernard Cassen, "Inventing ATTAC," in *A Movement of Movements*, ed. Tom Mertes, 152–74 (London: Verso, 2004).

40. Jeremy Brecher, Tim Costello, and Brendan Smith, *Globalization from Below* (Boston: South End, 2000), 64, 67.

41. Alliance for Responsible Trade, *A Just and Sustainable Trade and Development Initiative for the Western Hemisphere* (Washington, DC: ART, 1994). In addition to the umbrella groups responsible for producing the Initiative—Alliance for Responsible Trade, Citizens Trade Campaign, and the Mexican Action Network on Free Trade—the statement was endorsed by the Action Canada Network, Border Ecology Project, Development GAP, Greenpeace (U.S.), Institute for Policy Studies, Instituto Latinoamericano de Servicios Legales Alternativos (Colombia), Inter-Hemispheric Resource Center (Albuquerque), International Labor Rights Fund, National Consumers League, Resource Center of the Americas (Minneapolis), United Electrical Workers (UE), United Methodist Church, and others. In addition, the drafters of the Initiative acknowledged significant input from the Canadian Center for Policy Alternatives, the Center of Concern, the Alternative-Women in Development working group (Alt-WID), the Economic Policy Institute, and a variety of other groups and institutions that may not have been directly represented at the July 1992 meeting in Mexico City where the document was promulgated.

42. Alliance for Responsible Trade, *Just and Sustainable Trade,* 3–4.

43. Alliance for Responsible Trade, *Just and Sustainable Trade,* 5.

44. Rachel Kamel and Anya Hoffman, *The Maquiladora Reader* (Philadelphia: American Friends Service Committee, 1999), 114–15; compare Alliance for Responsible Trade, *Just and Sustainable Trade.*

45. Jeremy Brecher and Brendan Smith, "In Focus: The Global Sustainable Development Resolution," *Foreign Policy in Focus* (April 2000), at www.fpif.org/briefs/vol4/v4n12gsdr.html (accessed September 7, 2004); Bernie Sanders, *Global Sustainable Development Resolution* (Washington, DC: U.S. Congress, 1999).

46. Sanders, *Global Sustainable Development Resolution*, 2.

47. Sanders, *Global Sustainable Development Resolution*, 9.

48. Sanders, *Global Sustainable Development Resolution*, 16.

49. Sanders, *Global Sustainable Development Resolution*, 41.

50. Barlow and Clarke, *Global Showdown,* 170.

51. Barlow and Clarke, *Global Showdown,* 172, 175

52. Barlow and Clarke, *Global Showdown,* 207–8.

53. George Monbiot, *Age of Consent* (London: Flamingo Books, 2003), 53. For a formidable argument that global social justice is best pursued through increasing, rather than decreasing, trade, see Gavin Kitching, *Seeking Social Justice Through Globalization* (University Park: Pennsylvania State University Press, 2001).

54. Monbiot, *Age of Consent,* 4.

55. Monbiot, *Age of Consent,* 41.

56. Grahame Thompson, "Age of Confusion," *Open Democracy* (September 25, 2003): 2, at www.opendemocracy.net.

57. Thompson, "Age of Confusion," 6.

58. Jim Davis, "This Is What Bureaucracy Looks Like: NGOs and Anti-Capitalism," in *The Battle of Seattle: The New Challenge to Capitalist Globalization*, ed. E Yuen, G. Katsiaficas, and D. Rose, 175–82 (New York: Soft Skull Press, 2001).

59. Michael Albert, "Anarchists," in *Anti-Capitalism: A Guide to the Movement*, ed. Emma Bircham and John Charlton, 323 (London: Bookmarks, 2001); preceding quotation from Albert, "Anarchists," 322.

60. Alex Callinicos, *An Anti-Capitalist Manifesto* (Cambridge: Polity, 2003), 140.

61. WSF Charter of Principles, quoted in Teivo Teivainen, "World Social Forum: What Should It Be When It Grows Up?" *Open Democracy* (July 10, 2003): 7, at www.opendemocracy.net.

62. William Fisher and Thomas Ponniah, *Another World Is Possible* (London: Zed, 2003), 6.

63. Teivainen, "World Social Forum," 7.

64. Quoted in Fisher and Ponniah, *Another World*, 349.

65. Fisher and Ponniah, *Another World*, 8–10.

66. Fisher and Ponniah, *Another World*, 13, emphasis in original.

Chapter 4: Gender, Class, and the Transnational Politics of Solidarity

1. Paul Hirst and Grahame Thompson, *Globalization in Question* (Cambridge: Polity, 1996), 26.

2. S. Castles and M. J. Miller, *The Age of Migration*, 3d ed. (New York: Guilford, 2003), 57.

3. H. Zlotnik, *The Global Dimensions of Female Migration* (Washington, DC: Migration Policy Institute), March 1, 2003.

4. For an excellent review of immigration and wage effects see G. DeFreitas, "Immigration, Inequality, and Policy Alternatives," in *Globalization and Progressive Economic Policy*, ed. D. Baker, G. Epstein, and R. Pollin, 337–56 (Cambridge: Cambridge University Press, 1998).

5. For discussion of economic, cultural, and racial nationalisms as these have figured in debates surrounding globalization, see M. Rupert, *Ideologies of Globalization* (London: Routledge, 2000); and M. Steger, *Globalism: The New Market Ideology* (Lanham, MD: Rowman & Littlefield, 2002).

6. Samuel Huntington, "The Hispanic Challenge," *Foreign Policy* (March/April 2004): 31, 30, 32.

7. World Bank, *Global Development Finance Report* (Washington, DC: World Bank, 2003), 157.

8. World Bank, *Global Development Finance*, 158.

9. Jagdish Bhagwati, *Free Trade Today* (Princeton, NJ: Princeton University Press, 2002), 12.

10. Philippine Overseas Employment Administration, at www.poea.gov.ph/docs/ofwStock2003.doc (accessed April 2, 2005).

11. A. Abrera-Mangahas, "Response to New Market Opportunities: The Case of the Overseas Employment Sector," Working Paper #89-11 (Philippine Institute for Development Studies, 1989), 3–8.

12. C. Chin, *In Service and Servitude* (New York: Columbia University Press, 1998), 94–124.

13. Philippine Overseas Employment Administration, 2004, at www.poea.gov .ph/html/bba2003.htm (accessed December 1, 2004).

14. POEA, *Philippine Overseas Employment Administration Annual Report* (2003), 19.

15. Christine Chin, *In Service and Servitude*; Rachel Parrenas, *Servants of Globalization* (Stanford, CA: Stanford University Press, 2001); Nicole Constable, *Maid to Order in Hong Kong* (Ithaca, NY: Cornell University Press, 1997); K. Chang and L. H. M. Ling, "Globalization and Its Intimate Other: Filipina Domestic Workers in Hong Kong," in *Gender and Global Restructuring*, ed. M. H. Marchand and A. S. Runyan, 27–43 (New York: Routledge, 2000).

16. Chin, *In Service and Servitude*, 14.

17. Constable, *Maid to Order*, 3–7.

18. J. Arnado, *Mistresses and Maids: Inequality Among Third World Women Wage Earners* (Manila, Philippines: De La Salle University Press, 2003), 171.

19. Parrenas, *Servants of Globalization*, 172–3.

20. For an excellent analysis of this ambivalence see Nicole Constable's discussion of Filipina domestic workers in Hong Kong in "At Home But Not At Home: Filipina Narratives of Ambivalent Returns," in *Filipinos in Global Migrations: At Home in the World*, ed. Filomeno V. Aguilar Jr. (Manila: Philippine Migration Research Network, 2002).

21. Maria Mies, *Patriarchy and Accumulation on a World Scale* (London: Zed Books, 1986), 117.

22. Andrew Ross, *No Sweat* (London: Verso, 1997), 88.

23. Aiwa Ong, *Flexible Citizenship: The Cultural Logics of Transnationality* (Durham, NC: Duke University Press, 1997); N. Iglesias-Prieto, *Beautiful Flowers of the Maquiladoras* (Austin: University of Texas Press, 1997); Mies, *Patriarchy and Accumulation*; M. Fernandez-Kelly, *For We are Sold, I and My People: Women and Industrialization in Mexico's Frontier* (Albany: State University of New York Press, 1983).

24. Rachel Kamel and Anya Hoffman, *The Maquiladora Reader* (Philadelphia: American Friends Service Committee, 1999); Iglesias-Prieto, *Beautiful Flowers*.

25. Iglesias-Prieto, *Beautiful Flowers*; Mies, *Patriarchy and Accumulation*.

26. Chin, *In Service and Servitude*; Constable, *Maid to Order*; Constable, "At Home But Not At Home"; Parrenas, *Servants of Globalization*.

27. Constable, "At Home But Not At Home"; also Constable, *Maid to Order*; Chin, *In Service and Servitude*; Parrenas, *Servants of Globalization*.

28. W. Asato, "Organizing for Empowerment: Experiences of Filipino Domestic Workers in Hong Kong," in *Filipino Diaspora: Demography, Social Networks, Empowerment, and Culture*, ed. M. Tsuda (Manila: Philippine Social Science Council, 2003), 58.

29. Asian Migrant Centre, *Asian Migrant Yearbook 2002–2003* (Hong Kong: Asian Migrant Centre, 2004), 140.

30. The progressive/radical left in the Philippines has strong divisions between

reformist and radical wings, and some of these divisions are reflected in particular organizations in Hong Kong and other locations with large numbers of Filipino migrant workers. However, these divisions do not seem to be an obstacle when organizing around clear threats to the interests of migrant workers, though they do create conflict with regard to long-term strategy.

31. Around the same time as the wage cut a government tax was levied on employers of domestic workers that made the amount paid to a domestic worker for a two-year contract roughly the same. It has been suggested that this was done to avoid levying a tax directly on the domestic workers as it may have contravened ILO/UN conventions forbidding discrimination against migrant workers (by taxing the income of a particular nationality differently); *Asian Migrant Yearbook 2002–2003*, 141.

32. At least in terms of merely sending remittance income to the Philippines. There are some ongoing attempts at developing savings clubs with connections to particular small-scale investments controlled by those willing to invest. One benefit of the savings clubs that use partner organizations in the Philippines is the socially conscious nature of the projects. For example, when a group of seafarers contacted Unlad Kabayan, an NGO based in the Philippines dedicated to encouraging savings and micro-development projects for OFWs, with the idea of investing their income in an arena for cockfighting, they were encouraged to instead put their money into an organic chicken farm.

33. Castles and Miller, *Age of Migration*, 168–69.

34. *Asian Migrant Yearbook 2002–2003.*

35. No doubt this was foremost in the mind of the Macapagal-Arroyo administration in its handling of the Angelo de la Cruz case discussed at the beginning of this chapter.

36. Castles and Miller, *Age of Migration,* 169.

37. This conception of states is generally traced to the Treaty of Westphalia, 1648. See chapter 2 for our understanding of the state.

38. Jorge Durand, *From Traitors to Heroes: 100 Years of Mexican Migration Policies* (Washington, DC: Migration Policy Institute, March 1, 2004), 3.

39. Ong, *Flexible Citizenship.*

Chapter 5: Globalization, Imperialism, and Terror

1. This is, of course, a strong statement, and some readers may react with incredulity; but this claim is no hyperbole. U.S. imperial history is replete with episodes of mass murder in which official U.S. policy was directly or indirectly implicated: for evidence relevant to the post–World War II era, see William Blum, *Killing Hope: US Military and CIA Interventions since World War II* (Monroe, ME: Common Courage Press, 1995); and Frederick Gareau, *State Terrorism and the United States* (Atlanta, GA: Clarity Press, 2004).

2. World Bank Data and Statistics online, n.d., at www.worldbank.org/data/countrydata/countrydata.html.

3. United Nations, *Human Development Report,* 2002, 19, at hdr.undp.org/reports/global/2002/en/ (accessed September 6, 2004).

4. American exceptionalism, articulating liberal individualism with a self-righteous and militant nationalism, has long-standing residence in popular common sense in the U.S. and has been profoundly influential in shaping U.S. foreign policy during its rise to global power. See Michael Hunt, *Ideology and U.S. Foreign Policy* (New Haven, CT: Yale University Press, 1987). On the role of exceptionalist ideology in globalization debates within the U.S., see Mark Rupert, *Ideologies of Globalization* (London: Routledge, 2000).

5. George W. Bush quoted in Doyle McManus, "The World Casts a Critical Eye on Bush's Style of Diplomacy," *Los Angeles Times,* March 3, 2003.

6. See Gabriel Kolko, *Confronting the Third World* (New York: Pantheon, 1988); Walter La Feber, *The American Age* (New York: Norton, 1989); and Blum, *Killing Hope.*

7. Winston Churchill quoted in Daniel Yergin, *The Prize: The Epic Quest for Oil, Money and Power* (New York: Simon & Schuster, 1991), 154.

8. Yergin, *Prize,* 150–56.

9. Yergin, *Prize,* 160–63.

10. Yergin, *Prize,* 204–5; also Simon Bromley, *American Hegemony and World Oil* (University Park: Pennsylvania State University Press, 1991), 95–98.

11. Yergin, *Prize,* 306–88.

12. Bromley, *American Hegemony,* 105.

13. NSC-68 reprinted in Ernest May, *American Cold War Strategy* (New York: St. Martin's, 1993), 26, 29.

14. NSC-68 in May, *Strategy,* 48; see also 29, 41–43, 46, 53–54, 73.

15. NSC-68 in May, *Strategy,* 26, 43.

16. Bromley, *American Hegemony,* 105–6.

17. Michael Klare, "Bush-Cheney Energy Strategy: Procuring the Rest of the World's Oil" Foreign Policy in Focus Special Report, January 2004, at www.fpif.org/papers/03petropol/politics_body.html (accessed August 29, 2004); also Yergin, *Prize,* 403–5.

18. Stephen Kinzer, *All the Shah's Men* (New York: Wiley, 2003).

19. Thomas Friedman, *The Lexus and the Olive Tree* (New York: Farrar, Straus & Giroux, 1999), 373.

20. See Rupert, *Ideologies,* ch. 3; Manfred Steger, *Globalism* (Lanham, MD: Rowman & Littlefield, 2002), ch. 3.

21. It is important to note that a minority of Muslims live in the Middle East, and an even smaller subset are Arabs. Nonetheless, because of the roots of Islam in Arabic history, culture, and language, the Arab world is disproportionately significant for the Muslim world more generally; see, for example, Malise Ruthven, *Islam in the World,* 2d ed. (Oxford: Oxford University Press, 2000).

22. Rashid Khalidi, *Resurrecting Empire* (Boston: Beacon, 2004).

23. John Esposito, *Unholy War: Terror in the Name of Islam* (Oxford: Oxford University Press, 2002), 83–84.

24. Esposito, *Unholy War*, 50–51.

25. Qutb quoted in Malise Ruthven, *A Fury for God: The Islamist Attack on America* (London: Granta, 2002), 86–87.

26. Qutb quoted in Ruthven, *Fury*, 86–87.

27. Qutb quoted in Esposito, *Unholy War*, 60.

28. Esposito, *Unholy War*, 60.

29. This sudden and massive redistribution of global wealth to Saudi Arabia and other oil-rich Gulf states was the genesis of the contract migration from the Philippines (discussed in chapter 4), as well as the petrodollar recycling in the form of sovereign debt, which laid the groundwork for the Third World debt crisis (discussed in chapter 2) that persists today. After the events of September 11 many commentators made sweeping comments about the Middle East and modernity. To the extent that there is an element of truth to the claim that oil-rich Gulf states have had a delayed encounter with modernity, it may have something to do with the fact that these societies have had the ability to subcontract large sectors of their economy, particularly those involving manual labor and particular technical skills, to temporary migrants.

30. Esposito, *Unholy War*, 108; see also Ruthven, *Fury*, 177.

31. Esposito, *Unholy War*; Ruthven, *Fury*; and Steve Coll, *Ghost Wars: The Secret History of the CIA, Afghanistan, and Bin Laden* (New York: Penguin, 2004).

32. Ruthven, *Fury*, 202; see also Coll, *Ghost Wars*.

33. World Islamic Front, *Jihad against Jews and Crusaders*, 1998, reproduced by Federation of American Scientists at www.fas.org/irp/world/para/docs/980223-fatwa.htm (accessed August 16, 2004).

34. World Islamic Front, *Jihad*.

35. Joanna Chung and Alex Halperin, "Arab Attitudes to U.S. Hardening," *Financial Times*, July 24, 2004.

36. Esposito, *Unholy War*, 153.

37. Mir Zohair Husain, *Global Islamic Politics*, 2d ed. (New York: Longman, 2003), 108.

38. Mahmood Mamdani, *Good Muslim, Bad Muslim: America, the Cold War, and the Roots of Terror* (New York: Pantheon, 2004).

39. Helpful background on the Bush doctrine includes David Armstrong, "Dick Cheney's Song of America: Drafting a Plan for Global Dominance," *Harper's* (October 2002): 76–83; Tom Barry and Jim Lobe, "US Foreign Policy: Attention, Right Face, Forward March," *Foreign Policy in Focus* (April 2002), at www.foreignpolicy-infocus.org/papers/02right/index.html; Barry and Lobe, "The Men Who Stole the Show," *Foreign Policy in Focus* (October 2002), at www.foreignpolicy-infocus.org/papers/02men/index.html; Larry Everest, *Oil, Power and Empire* (Monroe, ME.: Common Courage, 2003); Gary Dorrien, *Imperial Designs: Neoconservatism and the New Pax Americana* (London: Routledge, 2004); Stefan Halper and Jonathan Clarke, *America Alone: The Neo-Conservatives and the Global Order* (Cambridge: Cambridge University Press, 2004); James Mann, *Rise of the Vulcans: The History of Bush's War Cabinet* (New York: Viking, 2004).

40. In the U.S. political context, "neoconservative" refers to a political tendency that had its roots in a band of Cold War liberals who became increasingly disillusioned with welfare state policies and the perceived influence of the anti–Vietnam War McGovernite wing within the Democratic Party and gravitated toward militantly anticommunist, free-market political positions overlapping (if not entirely congruent) with the emergent New Right of the 1970s and 1980s. As a result of this ideological confluence, the neocons shared in the largesse of strategically targeted conservative funding from the likes of the Bradley, Scaife, and Olin foundations and became part of the Reagan revolution. The influence of the neocons was especially pronounced in Reagan's actively anticommunist foreign policy. "Neoconservatives believed in the role of the United States as world leader: the defeat of communism was a first step toward spreading American-style 'democracy' around the world," Sara Diamond, *Roads to Dominion: Right-Wing Movements and Political Power in the US* (New York: Guilford, 1995), 275. For overviews of neoconservatism and accounts of how second-generation neocons came to exert such great influence over U.S. foreign policy in the second Bush administration, see Dorrien, *Imperial Designs*, and Halper and Clarke, *America Alone*.

41. PNAC, *Statement of Principles* (Washington, DC: Project for a New American Century, 1997), at: www.newamericancentury.org/statementofprinciples.htm.

42. It is noteworthy (especially in a Gramscian view) that PNAC has connections to conservative organizations waging the "culture wars" on American campuses, such as Lynne Cheney's American Council of Trustees and Alumni (www.goacta.org), William Bennett's Americans for Victory over Terrorism (www.avot.org), and Daniel Pipes's Campus Watch (www.campus-watch.org). Their leading personas are drawn from the incestuous tangle of right-wing political networks, the ideological visions they project are very nearly congruent, and they are funded by the notorious troika of ultraconservative and strategically deliberate foundations: Bradley, Scaife, and Olin (on which, see the data collected by the Media Transparency project, www.mediatransparecy.org). In the wake of 9/11, these organizations have sought to pressure insufficiently loyal U.S. academics into eschewing critical reexamination of America's role in the world and instead to reaffirm what they refer to as "traditional Western values," which are understood to be embodied in the U.S. and for which U.S. foreign policy is seen as a powerful evangelical vehicle. See, for example, Jerry Martin and Ann Neal, *Defending Civilization: How Our Universities Are Failing America and What Can Be Done about It* (Washington, DC: American Council of Trustees and Alumni, November 2001).

43. PNAC, quoted in Barry and Lobe, "Men Who Stole the Show," 2.

44. William Kristol and Robert Kagan, "Introduction: National Interest and Global Responsibility," in *Present Dangers,* ed. R. Kagan and W. Kristol, 6, 13, 23, 24 (San Francisco: Encounter Books, 2000). We should pause briefly to note that the principles enunciated in the *Declaration* do not originate with that document but derive largely from the English liberal philosopher John Locke.

45. Gary Schmidt quoted in Bruce Murphy, "Neoconservative Clout Seen in US Iraq Policy," *Milwaukee Journal-Sentinel,* April 3, 2003. Note that Schmidt is draw-

ing on an ascendant orthodoxy within American international relations scholarship—the so-called democratic peace thesis—to rationalize PNAC's neoimperial project. For a critique of the democratic peace thesis that broadens into a critical examination of the politics of American political science more generally, see Ido Oren, *Our Enemies and Us* (Ithaca, NY: Cornell University Press, 2003).

46. PNAC, *Letter to President George W. Bush* (Washington, DC: Project for a New American Century, January 23, 2003), at www.newamericancentury.org/Bushletter-012303.htm.

47. While not a charter member, Zoellick's signature appears beneath several PNAC advocacy letters including the 1998 statement pushing for a unilateral military solution in Iraq, available at www.newamericancentury.org/lettersstatements.htm.

48. White House, *National Security Strategy for the United States,* September 17, 2002, 1–2, at www.whitehouse.gov/nsc/print/nssall.html.

49. White House, *National Security Strategy*, 1, 21.

50. Military spending data from the Center for Defense Information, Washington, DC, n.d., at www.cdi.org/budget/2004/world-military-spending.cfm.

51. PNAC, *Letter to Bush.*

52. "Bush: Don't Wait for Mushroom Cloud." Transcript of speech given in Cincinnati, Ohio, October 6, 2002, at archives.cnn.com/2002/ALLPOLITICS/10/07/bush.transcript. On the Bush administration's dishonesty in regard to Iraq, see John Judis and Spencer Ackerman, "The Selling of the Iraq War," *The New Republic* (June 30, 2003): 14–25; Robert Dreyfuss and Jason Vest, "The Lie Factory," *Mother Jones* (January–February 2004): 34–41; David Sarota and Christy Harvey, "They Knew," *In These Times,* August 4, 2004; David Barstow, William Broad, and Jeff Gerth, "How the White House Embraced Disputed Arms Intelligence," *New York Times,* October 3, 2004; and Henry Waxman, *Iraq on the Record: The Bush Administration's Public Statements on Iraq,* United States House of Representatives, Committee on Government Reform, Minority Staff, Special Investigations Division, March, 16, 2004, at democrats.reform.house.gov/IraqOnTheRecord/.

53. Steven Kull, "Misperceptions, the Media, and the Iraq War" (research report, Program on International Policy Attitudes, University of Maryland, 2003), 8.

54. D. Kirkpatrick, "Mr. Murdoch's War," *New York Times,* April 7, 2003; Halper and Clarke, *America Alone,* 182–96. Note that in addition to owning Fox and a number of other influential media properties around the world, Rupert Murdoch is a major financial sponsor of PNAC founder William Kristol and his neoconservative journal, *The Weekly Standard.* The small-circulation magazine loses about $1 million a year, but has been influential within the Bush administration and is heavily subsidized by Murdoch. D. Carr, "White House Listens When Weekly Speaks," *New York Times,* March 11, 2003.

55. Kull, "Misperceptions," quotations from 2, 7, 12, 9. Using classic social science methods, the study's authors "controlled for" demographic differences by comparing percentages of respondents *within* particular demographic categories. In this way, they were able to demonstrate that belief in these pivotal misconcep-

tions was not attributable to the demographic characteristics of different networks' audiences ("Misperceptions," 15–16).

56. Quoted in Peter Johnson, "Amanpour: CNN Practiced Self-Censorship," *USA Today,* September 15, 2003.

57. Michael Massing, "Now They Tell Us," *New York Review of Books,* February 26, 2004, 9, at www.nybooks.com/articles/169222004.

58. *New York Times,* "A Pause for Hindsight," July 16, 2004; Howard Kurtz, "The Post on WMDs: An Inside Story," *Washington Post,* August 12, 2004; compare Massing, "Now They Tell Us."

59. As John Judis has noted, Iraq is not the first American military occupation in the guise of "liberation." When President Bush visited the Philippines in October 2003, he gave the Philippine Congress a Bush-style history lesson: "Together our soldiers liberated the Philippines from colonial rule," Bush told the Filipino legislators. He went on to draw parallels between the U.S. bringing democracy to the Philippines and the U.S. project of bringing democracy to the Middle East. "As many Philippine commentators remarked afterward," Judis observed, "Bush's rendition of Philippine-American history bore little relation to fact. True, the US Navy ousted Spain from the Philippines in the Spanish-American War of 1898. But instead of creating a Philippine democracy, the McKinley administration, its confidence inflated by victory in that 'splendid little war,' annexed the country and installed a colonial administrator. The United States then waged a brutal war against the same Philippine independence movement it encouraged to fight against Spain. The war dragged on for 14 years. Before it ended, about 120,000 U.S. troops were deployed, more than 4,000 were killed, and more than 200,000 Filipino civilians and soldiers were killed. Resentment lingered a century later during Bush's visit." John Judis, "Imperial Amnesia," *Foreign Policy* (July–August, 2004): 50–52. The point, of course, is that we unlearn such history at our peril. That the U.S. commander-in-chief was so blithely unaware of the irony involved in comparing the Iraq war to the Philippine Insurrection, and the possible implications of such a comparison, should be disturbing.

60. United States Department of Energy, *Energy Information Administration Petroleum Supply Annual* 2003, Table 29, at www.eia.doe.gov/neic/quickfacts/quick oil.html.

61. See Robert Dreyfuss, "The Thirty-Year Itch," *Mother Jones* (March 1, 2003): 40–45; John Judis, "Over a Barrel: Who Will Control Iraq's Oil?" *The New Republic* (January 20, 2003): 20–23; Michael Klare, "Bush-Cheney Energy Strategy: Procuring the Rest of the World's Oil," *Foreign Policy in Focus Special Report,* January 2004, at www.fpif.org/papers/03petropol/politics_body.html2004.

62. See, for example, Martin Carnoy, *The State and Political Theory* (Princeton, NJ: Princeton University Press, 1984).

63. Antonio Gramsci, *Selections from the Prison Notebooks* (New York: International Publishers, 1971), 162, 164, 377.

64. Dreyfuss, "Thirty-Year Itch."

65. Quotations from White House, *National Security Strategy,* 13, 1, 12.

66. White House, *National Security Strategy*, 12.

67. Leo Panitch and Sam Gindin, "Global Capitalism and American Empire," in *Socialist Register: The New Imperial Challenge*, ed. L. Panitch and S. Gindin, 22 (London: Merlin, 2003).

68. Howard LaFranchi, "The World's View of US," *Christian Science Monitor*, March 17, 2004, 4.

69. First quotation from Joshua Marshall, "Kerry Faces the World," *Atlantic Monthly* (July–August, 2004): 112; Democratic Party platform quoted in Stephen Zunes, "Democratic Party Platform Shows Shift to the Right on Foreign Policy," *Foreign Policy in Focus* (August 5, 2004): 1, at www.fpif.org/commentary/2004/0408shift.html.

Conclusion

1. Zapatistas, *Documents from the 1996 Encounter for Humanity and against Neoliberalism* (New York: Seven Stories Press, 1998), 47, 45.

BIBLIOGRAPHY

Abrera-Mangahas, A. "Response to New Market Opportunities: The Case of the Overseas Employment Sector." Working Paper #89-11. Manila: Philippine Institute for Development Studies, 1989.

Agnew, John, and Stuart Corbridge. *Mastering Space*. London: Routledge, 1995.

Albert, Michael. "Anarchists." In *Anti-Capitalism: A Guide to the Movement*, edited by Emma Bircham and John Charlton, 321–27. London: Bookmarks, 2001.

Alliance for Responsible Trade. *A Just and Sustainable Trade and Development Initiative for the Western Hemisphere*. Washington, DC: ART, 1994.

Anti-Capitalist Convergence. *Why We Are Not Making Demands of the World Economic Forum*. New York: ACC, 2002, at www.accnyc.org/issues_wef demands.html.

Armstrong, David. "Dick Cheney's Song of America: Drafting a Plan for Global Dominance." *Harper's* (October 2002): 76–83.

Arnado, J. *Mistresses and Maids: Inequality Among Third World Women Wage Earners*. Manila, Philippines: De La Salle University Press, 2003.

Asato, W. "Organizing for Empowerment: Experiences of Filipino Domestic Workers in Hong Kong." In *Filipino Diaspora: Demography, Social Networks, Empowerment, and Culture*, edited by M. Tsuda, 41–66. Manila, Philippines: Philippine Social Science Council, 2003.

Asian Migrant Centre. *Asian Migrant Yearbook 2002–2003*. Hong Kong: Asian Migrant Centre, 2004.

Barrett, Michele. *Women's Oppression Today*. Rev. ed. London: Verso, 1988.

Barlow, Maude, and Tony Clarke. *Global Showdown*. Toronto: Stoddart Publishing, 2002.

Barry, Dan. "Appearing in the Role of Evil: The Other Side." *New York Times*, January 31, 2002.

Barry, Tom, and Jim Lobe. "The Men Who Stole the Show." *Foreign Policy in Focus* (October 2002), at www.foreignpolicy-infocus.org/papers/02men/index.html.

———. "US Foreign Policy: Attention, Right Face, Forward March." *Foreign Policy in Focus* (April 2002), at www.foreignpolicy-infocus.org/papers/02right/index.html.

Bello, Walden. *Dark Victory*. London: Pluto, 1994.

Bhagwati, Jagdish. *Free Trade Today*. Princeton, NJ: Princeton University Press, 2002.

Block, Fred. "The Ruling Class Does Not Rule." *Socialist Revolution* 33 (May–June, 1977): 6–28.

Blum, William. *Killing Hope: US Military and CIA Interventions since World War II*. Monroe, ME: Common Courage Press, 1995.

Bookchin, Murray. *The Murray Bookchin Reader*. Edited by Janet Biehl. London: Cassell, 1997.

Bowles, Samuel, and Herbert Gintis. *Democracy and Capitalism*. New York: Basic, 1986.

Brecher, Jeremy, and Brendan Smith. "The Global Sustainable Development Resolution." *Foreign Policy in Focus* (April 2000), at www.fpif.org/briefs/vol4/v4n12gsdr.html (accessed September 7, 2004).

Brecher, Jeremy, Tim Costello, and Brendan Smith. *Globalization from Below*. Boston, South End, 2000.

Brenner, Robert. *The Boom and the Bubble: The US in the World Economy*. London: Verso, 2002.

———. "The Social Basis of Economic Development." In *Analytical Marxism*, edited by J. Roemer, 23–53. Cambridge: Cambridge University Press, 1986.

Bromley, Simon. *American Hegemony and World Oil*. University Park: Pennsylvania State University Press, 1991.

Bronfenbrenner, Kate. "We'll Close!" *Multinational Monitor* 18, no. 3 (March 1997), at www.essential.org/monitor/hyper/mm0397.04.html.

———. "Raw Power." *Multinational Monitor* 21, no. 12 (December 2000), at, www.essential.org/monitor/mm2000/00december/power.html.

Buchanan, Patrick. *The Great Betrayal*. Boston: Little, Brown, 1998.

Callinicos, Alex. *An Anti-Capitalist Manifesto*. Cambridge: Polity, 2003.

Carnoy, Martin. *The State and Political Theory*. Princeton, NJ: Princeton University Press, 1984.

Carr, David. "White House Listens When Weekly Speaks." *New York Times,* March 11, 2003.

Cassen, Bernard. "Inventing ATTAC." In *A Movement of Movements*, edited by Tom Mertes, 152–74. London: Verso, 2004.

Castells, Manuel. *The Power of Identity*. Oxford: Blackwell, 1997.

Castles, S., and M. J. Miller *The Age of Migration*. 3d ed. New York: Guilford, 2003.

Chang, K. A., and L. H. M. Ling. "Globalization and Its Intimate Other: Fili-pina Domestic Workers in Hong Kong." In *Gender and Global Restructur-ing*, edited by M. H. Marchand and A. S. Runyan, 27–43. New York: Routledge, 2000.

Chin, C. *In Service and Servitude*. New York: Columbia University Press, 1998.

Chomsky, Noam. "Introduction." In *Anarchism*, by Daniel Guerin, vii–xx. New York: Monthly Review Press, 1970.

Chung, Joanna, and Alex Halperin. "Arab Attitudes to US Hardening." *Finan-cial Times*, July 24, 2004.

Cleaver, Harry. *The Chiapas Uprising and the Future of Class Struggle in the New World Order*, 1994, at www.eco.utexas.edu/facstaff/Cleaver/chiapasuprising .html.

Coll, Steve. *Ghost Wars: The Secret History of the CIA, Afghanistan, and Bin Laden*. New York: Penguin, 2003.

Constable, Nicole. "At Home But Not At Home: Filipina Narratives of Ambiva-lent Returns." In *Filipinos in Global Migrations: At Home in the World*, ed-ited by Filomeno V. Aguilar Jr., 380–412. Manila: Philippine Migration Research Network, 2002.

———. *Maid to Order in Hong Kong*. Ithaca, NY: Cornell University Press, 1997.

Cox, Robert. *Approaches to World Order*. Cambridge: Cambridge University Press, 1996.

———. *Production, Power, and World Order*. New York: Columbia University Press, 1987.

Davis, Jim. "This Is What Bureaucracy Looks Like: NGOs and Anti-Capital-ism." In *The Battle of Seattle: The New Challenge to Capitalist Globalization*, edited by E. Yuen, G. Katsiaficas, and D. Rose, 175–82. New York: Soft Skull Press, 2001.

de Jonquieres, Guy, and Holly Yeager. "Davos Goes West." *Financial Times*, Jan-uary 30, 2002.

DeFreitas, G. "Immigration, Inequality, and Policy Alternatives." In *Globaliza-tion and Progressive Economic Policy*, edited by D. Baker, G. Epstein, and R. Pollin, 337–56. Cambridge: Cambridge University Press, 1998.

Diamond, Sara. *Roads to Dominion: Right-Wing Movements and Political Power in the US*. New York: Guilford,1995

Dicken, Peter. *Global Shift*. 2d ed. New York: Guilford, 1992.

Dorrien, Gary. *Imperial Designs: Neoconservatism and the New Pax Americana*. London: Routledge, 2004.

Dreyfuss, Robert. "The Thirty-Year Itch." *Mother Jones*, March 1, 2003, at www.motherjones.com/news/feature/2003/10/ma_273_01.html.

Dreyfuss, Robert, and Jason Vest. "The Lie Factory." *Mother Jones* (January–February 2004): 34–41.

Durand, J. "From Traitors to Heroes: 100 Years of Mexican Migration Policies." Washington, DC: Migration Policy Institute, March 1, 2004, at www .migrationinformation.org/Feature/display.cfm?ID = 203.

Enloe, Cynthia. *Bananas, Beaches and Bases.* Berkeley: University of California Press, 1989.

Epstein, Barbara. "Anarchism and the Anti-Globalization Movement." *Monthly Review,* September 2001, at www.monthlyreview.org/0901epstein.htm.

Escobar, Arturo. *Encountering Development.* Princeton, NJ: Princeton University Press, 1995.

Esposito, John. *Unholy War: Terror in the Name of Islam.* Oxford: Oxford University Press, 2002.

Everest, Larry. *Oil, Power and Empire.* Monroe, ME.: Common Courage, 2003.

Featherstone, Liza. *Students Against Sweatshops.* London: Verso, 2002.

Fernandez-Kelly, M. P. *For We Are Sold, I and My People: Women and Industrialization in Mexico's Frontier.* Albany: State University of New York Press, 1983.

Finnegan, William. "After Seattle: Anarchists Get Organized." *The New Yorker* (April 17, 2000): 40–51.

Fisher, William, and Thomas Ponniah. *Another World Is Possible.* London: Zed, 2003.

Friedman, Thomas. *The Lexus and the Olive Tree.* New York: Farrar, Straus & Giroux, 2000.

———. "Senseless in Seattle." *New York Times,* December 1, 1999.

Gareau, Frederick. *State Terrorism and the United States.* Atlanta, GA: Clarity Press, 2004.

Gordon, David. *Fat and Mean.* New York: Free Press, 1996.

Graeber, David. "Anarchy in the USA." *In These Times,* January 10, 2000, at www.inthesetimes.com/.

———. "The New Anarchists." In *A Movement of Movements,* edited by Tom Mertes, 202–15. London: Verso, 2004.

———. "Reinventing Democracy." *In These Times,* February 19, 2002, at www.inthesetimes.com/.

Gramsci, Antonio. *Selections from the Prison Notebooks.* New York: International Publishers, 1971.

Graz, Jean-Christophe. "How Powerful Are Transnational Elite Clubs? The Social Myth of the World Economic Forum." *New Political Economy* 8, no. 3 (2003): 321–40.

Greider, William. *One World, Ready or Not.* New York: Simon & Schuster, 1997.

Hahnel, Robin. *Panic Rules.* Boston: South End, 1999.

Hall, Stuart. "The West and the Rest: Discourse and Power." In *Modernity,* edited by S. Hall, D. Held, D. Hubert, and K. Thompson, 184–227. Oxford: Blackwell, 1996.

Halper, Stefan, and Jonathan Clarke. *America Alone: The Neo-Conservatives and the Global Order.* Cambridge: Cambridge University Press, 2004.

Harding, James. "Counter Capitalism: Inside the Black Bloc." *Financial Times,* October 15, 2001, at specials.ft.com/countercap/FT3BG4GLUSC.html.

Hardt, Michael, and Antonio Negri. "What the Protesters in Genoa Want." *New York Times,* July 20, 2001.

Harvey, David. *The Condition of Postmodernity.* Oxford: Blackwell, 1989.

Heilbroner, Robert. *Marxism: For and Against.* New York: Norton, 1980.

Held, David, A. McGrew, D. Goldblatt, and J. Perraton. *Global Transformations.* Cambridge: Polity, 1999.

Henwood, Doug. "Wealth News." *Left Business Observer* 94 (May 5, 2000): n.p.

Hirst, Paul, and Grahame Thompson. *Globalization in Question.* Cambridge: Polity, 1996.

Hochschild, Adam. *King Leopold's Ghost.* Boston: Houghton Mifflin, 1998.

Hollingdale, Michael. "NGOs Threaten Forum Withdrawal." *Swiss Info,* January 28, 2001, at www.swissinfo.org.

Hunt, Michael. *Ideology and US Foreign Policy.* New Haven, CT: Yale University Press, 1987.

Huntington, Samuel. "The Hispanic Challenge." *Foreign Policy* (March/April 2004): 30–45.

Husain, Mir Zohair. *Global Islamic Politics.* 2d ed. New York: Longman, 2003.

Iglesias-Prieto, N. *Beautiful Flowers of the Maquiladoras.* Austin: University of Texas Press, 1997.

Irwin, Douglas. *Free Trade under Fire.* Princeton, NJ: Princeton University Press, 2002.

Johnson, Peter. "Amanpour: CNN Practiced Self-Censorship." *USA Today,* September 15, 2003.

———. "Imperial Amnesia." *Foreign Policy* (July/August 2004): 50–59.

———. "Over a Barrel: Who Will Control Iraq's Oil?" *The New Republic* (January 20, 2003): 20–23.

Judis, John, and Spencer Ackerman. "The Selling of the Iraq War." *The New Republic* (June 30, 2003): 14–25.

Kamel, Rachel, and Anya Hoffman. *The Maquiladora Reader.* Philadelphia: American Friends Service Committee, 1999.

Kaplan, Esther. "Keepers of the Flame." *Village Voice,* January 29, 2002, at www.villagevoice.com/issues/0205/kaplan.php.

Keynes, John Maynard. *The Economic Consequences of the Peace.* New York: Penguin, 1995.

Khalidi, Rashid. *Resurrecting Empire.* Boston: Beacon, 2004.

Kirkpatrick, David. "Mr. Murdoch's War." *New York Times,* April 7, 2003.

Klare, Michael. "Bush-Cheney Energy Strategy: Procuring the Rest of the World's Oil." *Foreign Policy in Focus,* January 2004, at www.fpif.org/papers/03petropol/politics_body.html.

Klein, Naomi. "Reclaiming the Commons." In *A Movement of Movements*, edited by Tom Mertes, 219–29. London: Verso, 2004.

———. "The Vision Thing." In *The Battle of Seattle*, edited by E. Yuen, G. Katsiaficas, and D. Rose, 311–18. New York: Soft Skull Press, 2001.

Kolko, Gabriel. *Confronting the Third World.* New York: Pantheon, 1988.

Kristol, William, and Robert Kagan. "Introduction: National Interest and Global Responsibility." In *Present Dangers*, edited by R. Kagan and W. Kristol, 3–24. San Francisco: Encounter Books, 2000.

Krugman, Paul. "In Praise of Cheap Labor." *Slate,* March 20, 1997, at web.mit.edu/krugman/www/smokey.html.

Kull, Steven. "Misperceptions, the Media, and the Iraq War." Program on International Policy Attitudes: University of Maryland, 2003.

Kurtz, Howard. "The Post on WMDs: An Inside Story." *Washington Post,* August 12, 2004.

LaBotz, Dan. "Moving for Global Justice." *Against the Current* 88 (September–October 2000), at www.igc.org/solidarity/atc.

LaFeber, Walter. *The American Age.* New York: Norton, 1989.

LaFranchi, Howard. "The World's View of US." *Christian Science Monitor* (March 17, 2004): n.p.

Mamdani, Mahmood. *Good Muslim, Bad Muslim: America, the Cold War, and the Roots of Terror.* New York: Pantheon, 2004.

Mann, James. *Rise of the Vulcans: The History of Bush's War Cabinet.* New York: Viking, 2004.

Marcos. *Our Word Is Our Weapon.* New York: Seven Stories Press, 2001.

Martin, Jerry, and Anne Neal. *Defending Civilization: How Our Universities Are Failing America and What Can Be Done about It.* Washington, DC: American Council of Trustees and Alumni, November 2001.

Marshall, Joshua. "Kerry Faces the World." *Atlantic Monthly* (July–August, 2004): 108–14.

Marx, Karl. *Capital.* Volume 1. New York: Vintage, 1977.

———. "Economic and Philosophical Manuscripts." In *Karl Marx: Early Writings,* 279–400. London: Penguin, 1975.

———. *The 18th Brumaire of Louis Bonaparte.* New York: International Publishers, 1991.

———. "The German Ideology." In *Karl Marx: Selected Writings*, edited by D. McLellan, 175–208. Oxford: Oxford University Press, 2000.

Marx, Karl, and Frederick Engels. "The Communist Manifesto." In *Karl Marx: Selected Writings,* edited by D. McLellan, 245–72. Oxford: Oxford University Press, 2000.

Massing, Michael. "Now They Tell Us." *New York Review of Books,* February 26, 2004, at www.nybooks.com/articles/16922.

McLean, Charles. "The Case for Davos." *International Herald Tribune,* February 13, 2001.

McManus, Doyle. "The World Casts a Critical Eye on Bush's Style of Diplomacy." *Los Angeles Times,* March 3, 2003.

McNally, David. "Mass Protests in Quebec City: From Anti-Globalization to Anti-Capitalism." *New Politics* 8, no. 3 (2001): 76–86.

Mies, Maria. *Patriarchy and Accumulation on a World Scale.* London: Zed Books, 1986.

Monbiot, George. *Age of Consent.* London: Flamingo Books, 2003.

Moody, Kim. *An Injury to All: The Decline of American Unionism.* London: Verso, 1988.

———. *Workers in a Lean World.* London: Verso, 1997.

Murphy, Bruce. "Neoconservative Clout Seen in US Iraq Policy." *Milwaukee Journal-Sentinel,* April 3, 2003.

New York Times. "A Pause for Hindsight," July 16, 2004.

Ollman, Bertell. *Dance of the Dialectic.* Urbana: University of Illinois Press, 2003.

Ong, Aiwa. *Flexible Citizenship: The Cultural Logics of Transnationality.* Durham, NC: Duke University Press, 1997.

———. *Spirits of Resistance and Capitalist Discipline.* Albany: State University of New York Press, 1987.

Oren, Ido. *Our Enemies and Us.* Ithaca, NY: Cornell University Press, 2003.

Panitch, Leo, and Sam Gindin. "Global Capitalism and American Empire." In *Socialist Register: The New Imperial Challenge,* edited by L. Panitch and S. Gindin, 1–42. London: Merlin, 2003.

Parreñas, R. S. *Servants of Globalization.* Stanford, CA: Stanford University Press, 2001.

Peterson, V. Spike. *A Critical Rewriting of Global Political Economy.* London: Routledge, 2003.

Pettman, Jan. *Worlding Women.* London: Routledge, 1996.

POEA. *Philippine Overseas Employment Administration Annual Report 2003,* at www.poea.gov.ph.

Project for a New American Century. *Statement of Principles.* Washington, DC: Project for a New American Century, June 3, 1997, at www.newamerican century.org/statementofprinciples.htm.

———. *Letter to President George W. Bush.* Washington, DC: Project for a New American Century, January 23, 2003, at www.newamericancentury.org/ Bushletter-012303.htm.

Public Citizen/Global Trade Watch. *Davos World Economic Forum: Pricey Corporate Trade Association Loses Its Camouflage.* Washington, DC: Public Citizen, 2002.

Reich, Robert. *The Work of Nations.* New York: Addison-Wesley, 1991.

Ross, Andrew. *No Sweat.* London: Verso, 1997.

Ross, John. *The War Against Oblivion.* Monroe, ME: Common Courage, 2000.

Rupert, Mark. "Globalizing Common Sense: A Marxian-Gramscian (Re-)vision of the Politics of Governance/Resistance." *Review of International Studies* 29 (2003): 181–98.

———. *Ideologies of Globalization.* London: Routledge, 2000.

———. *Producing Hegemony.* Cambridge: Cambridge University Press, 1995.

Ruthven, Malise. *A Fury for God: The Islamist Attack on America.* London: Granta, 2002.

———. *Islam in the World.* 2d ed. Oxford: Oxford University Press, 2000.

Sanders, Bernie. *Global Sustainable Development Resolution.* Washington, DC: U.S. Congress, 1999.

Sarota, David, and Christy Harvey. "They Knew." *In These Times,* August 4, 2004.

Sayer, Derek. *Capitalism and Modernity.* London: Routledge, 1991.

Schmitt, Richard. *Introduction to Marx and Engels.* 2d ed. Boulder, CO: Westview, 1997.

Schwab, Klaus. *Finding the Right Balance: Opening Address to Annual Meeting.* Davos: World Economic Forum, 1999, at live99.weforum.org/opening _ksc.asp.

Schwab, Klaus, and Claude Smadja. "Start Taking the Backlash Against Globalization Seriously." *International Herald Tribune,* February 1, 1996.

———. "Globalization Needs a Human Face." *International Herald Tribune,* January 28, 1999.

Smith, Adam. *Wealth of Nations.* Edited by K. Sutherland. Oxford: Oxford University Press, 1993.

Steger, Manfred. *Globalism: The New Market Ideology.* Lanham, MD: Rowman & Littlefield, 2002.

Stiglitz, Joseph. *Globalization and Its Discontents.* New York: Norton, 2002.

Strom, Stephanie, and Louis Uchitelle. "Economic Forum Moves to Manhattan." *New York Times,* January 27, 2002.

Swardson, Anne. "Entrance Fees to the Marketplace of Ideas." *Washington Post,* January 24, 2000.

Teivainen, Teivo. "World Social Forum: What Should It Be When It Grows Up?" *Open Democracy,* July 10, 2003, at www.opendemocracy.net.

Thomas, Paul. *Alien Politics.* London: Routledge, 1994.

Thompson, Grahame. "Age of Confusion." *Open Democracy,* September 25, 2003, at www.opendemocracy.net.

Tyson, Laura. *Who's Bashing Whom?* Washington, DC: Institute for International Economics, 1992.

United Nations. *Human Development Report,* 2002, at hdr.undp.org/reports/ global/2002/en/ (accessed September 6, 2004).

United States Department of Energy, Energy Information Administration. *Petroleum Supply Annual 2003,* Table 29, at www.eia.doe.gov/neic/quickfacts/ quickoil.html.

van der Pijl, Kees. *Transnational Classes and International Relations*. London: Routledge, 1998.

Wachtel, Howard. *The Money Mandarins*. Armonk, NY: Sharpe, 1990.

Wallach, Lori, and Michelle Sforza. *Whose Trade Organization?* Washington, DC: Public Citizen/Global Trade Watch, 1999.

Waxman, Henry. *Iraq on the Record: The Bush Administration's Public Statements on Iraq*. United States House of Representatives, Committee on Government Reform, Minority Staff, Special Investigations Division, March 16, 2004, at democrats.reform.house.gov/IraqOnTheRecord.

White House. *National Security Strategy for the United States,* September 17, 2002, at www.whitehouse.gov/nsc/print/nssall.html.

Wood, Ellen. *Empire of Capital*. London: Verso, 2003.

———. *The Origin of Capitalism*. New York: Monthly Review Press, 1999.

World Bank. *Global Development Finance Report*. Washington. DC: World Bank, 2003.

———. *World Development Report 1995*. Oxford: Oxford University Press, 1995.

———. *World Development Report 2000–01,* at econ.worldbank.org/wdr/ (accesses).

World Economic Forum. *About the World Economic Forum*. Geneva: WEF, 1997.

———.*Committed to Improving the State of the World*. Geneva: WEF, 1997.

———.*Creative Impatience Can Manage Problems of Globalization*, February 1, 1996, at www.weforum.org/frames/press/am96/pr10ph.htm.

World Islamic Front. Jihad against Jews and Crusaders, February 23, 1998, reproduced by Federation of American Scientists, at www.fas.org/irp/world/para/docs/980223–fatwa.htm.

World Trade Organization. *Trading into the Future*. Geneva: WTO, 1995.

———. *Trading into the Future*. 2d ed. Geneva: WTO, 1998.

Yergin, Daniel. *The Prize: The Epic Quest for Oil, Money and Power*. New York: Simon & Schuster, 1991.

Zapatistas. *Documents from the 1996 Encounter for Humanity and against Neoliberalism*. New York: Seven Stories Press, 1998.

Zlotnik, H. *The Global Dimensions of Female Migration*. Washington, DC: Migration Policy Institute, March 1, 2003, at www.migrationinformation.org/Feature/display.cfm?ID = 109.

Zunes, Stephen. "Democratic Party Platform Shows Shift to the Right on Foreign Policy." *Foreign Policy in Focus*, August 5, 2004, at www.fpif.org/commentary/2004/0408shift.html.

INDEX

Afghanistan, 119
agriculture, 27
Albert, Michael, 77
al Qaeda, 119, 124
Amanpour, Christiane, 126
American Council of Trustees and
    Alumni, 152n42
American exceptionalism, 130, 150n4
Americanization, 6
Americans for Victory over Terrorism,
    152n42
Amnesty International, 69
anarchism, 64–69, 75, 78
Anglo-Iranian Oil Company, 113
Anglo-Persian Oil Company, 111
anti-Americanism, 120, 136
Anti-Capitalist Convergence, 67
anticapitalist movements, 22–23
antiglobalization, 6, 61–62. *See also*
    global justice movement
antiwar protests, 125
Arabian-American Oil Company
    (ARAMCO), 113
Arabs, 150n21
assembly lines, 36, 37
Association for the Taxation of Finan-
    cial Transactions for the Aid of Citi-
    zens (ATTAC), 71

autarky, 6
Azzam, Sheikh Abdullah, 119

Bagong Bayani Awards, 88
Bakunin, Mikhail, 65, 68
Barlow, Maude, 64, 74–75
Belgian Congo, 31
Bello, Walden, 47, 61
Bennett, William, 152n42
Bharatiya Janat Party (BJP), 23
bin Laden, Osama, 7, 119, 120, 130
Black Bloc, 66
bonds, 140n17
Bono, 61
Bookchin, Murray, 65–66
Bowles, Sam, 18
Bradley Foundation, 122, 152n42
Brecher, Jeremy, 71
Bretton Woods agreements, 39–40
Bretton Woods system, 40, 45–46
British Petroleum, 111
British Royal Navy, 111
Buchanan, Patrick, 1, 60, 105
Bush, George W., 87, 105, 109, 124,
    125, 154n59
Bush doctrine: misrepresentation of
    Iraq and Saddam Hussein, 124–26;

167

ABOUT THE AUTHORS

Mark Rupert is professor of political science at Syracuse University's Maxwell School of Citizenship and Public Affairs, where he teaches in the areas of international relations, political economy, and the political theories of Karl Marx and Antonio Gramsci. Mark's research focuses on the intersection of the U.S. political economy with global structures and processes. He is the author of *Producing Hegemony: The Politics of Mass Production and American Global Power* (1995) and *Ideologies of Globalization: Contending Visions of a New World Order* (2000). He is coeditor (with Hazel Smith) of *Historical Materialism and Globalization* (2002). Mark's home page can be found online at faculty.maxwell.syr.edu/merupert/merindex.htm.

M. Scott Solomon is assistant professor of government and international affairs at the University of South Florida (USF) and research fellow at the University of South Florida Globalization Research Center. His research interests include globalization, migration, and international political economy. Before joining USF he taught at the Graduate Program in International Affairs at New School University in New York City. After receiving his Ph.D. from the Maxwell School of Citizenship and Public Affairs at Syracuse University, he served as the Lingnan Foundation Teaching Scholar at Lingnan University, Hong Kong's liberal arts university. He is the coauthor of "Historical Materialism, Ideology, and the Politics of Globalizing Capitalism" in *Historical Materialism and Globalization*, edited by Mark Rupert and Hazel Smith, and has authored several articles for the *Routledge Encyclopedia of International Political Economy*.